Carnegie
Library of
Pittsburgh
Main

A FRONT ROW SEAT

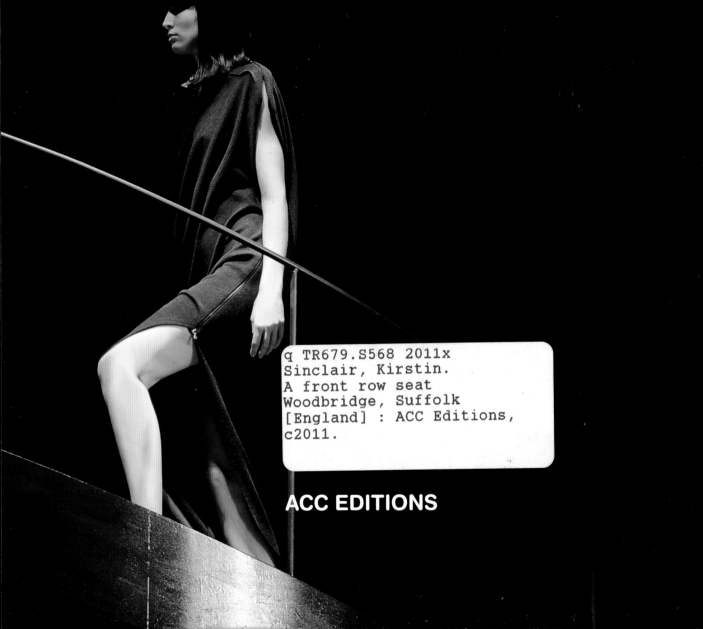

q TR679.S568 2011x
Sinclair, Kirstin.
A front row seat
Woodbridge, Suffolk
[England] : ACC Editions,
c2011.

ACC EDITIONS

© Kirstin Sinclair 2011

World copyright reserved

The right of Kirstin Sinclair to be identified as Author of this Work has been asserted by her in accordance with the Copyright, Designs and Patents Act 1988

Every effort has been made to secure all necessary permissions to reproduce images contained within this book. Any errors or omissions should be addressed to the publisher and will be corrected in later editions.

All rights reserved. No part of this publication may be reproduced, stored in a retrieval system, or transmitted in any form or by any means, electronic, mechanical, photocopying, recording or otherwise, without the prior permission in writing of the publisher, nor be otherwise circulated in any form or binding or cover other than that in which it is published and without a similar condition including this condition being imposed on the subsequent purchaser.

ISBN 978-1-85149-661-7

British Library Cataloguing-in-Publication Data
A catalogue record for this book is available from the British Library

Text: Kirstin Sinclair
Photography: Kirstin Sinclair (unless otherwise stated)

Printed and bound in Slovenia for ACC Editions, an imprint of the Antique Collectors' Club Ltd

Published in England by ACC Editions, an imprint of the Antique Collectors' Club Ltd
Sandy Lane, Old Martlesham
Woodbridge, Suffolk IP12 4SD, UK
Tel 01394 389950 Fax 01394 389999
Email info@antique-acc.com
www.antiquecollectorsclub.com

ACC Distribution
6 West 18th Street, Suite 4B
New York, NY 10011, USA
Tel 212 645 1111 Fax 212 989 3205
Email sales@antiquecc.com

Front cover: FRIDA GUSTAVSSON in the autumn/winter 2011 Alexander McQueen womenswear show; Paris, March 2011

page 1: The autumn/winter 2010 Alberta Ferretti womenswear show; Milan, February 2010

pages 2–3: FRIDA GUSTAVSSON in the autumn/winter 2010 Lanvin womenswear show; Paris, March 2010

pages 4–5: DAIANE CONTERATO in the autumn/winter 2010 Ann Demeulemeester womenswear show; Paris, March 2010

Back cover: KARLIE KLOSS in the autumn/winter 2008 Rodarte womenswear show; New York, February 2008 (photograph features in the 'Catwalk to Cover' exhibition organised by the Fashion and Textile Museum, London)

Back cover (detail): The spring/summer 2010 G-Star show; New York, September 2009

contents

foreword

WITH THE PROLIFERATION OF IMAGES from the catwalk featuring across all forms of media over the last 10 to 15 years, photographs of models appearing to effortlessly glide down the runway have become part of our daily fashion fodder. Firsthand experience of the industry tells me that there is much more to this than first meets the eye, however.

From the frenetic backstage to the star-studded front row, every aspect of a catwalk show and the images from it embodies meticulous preparation and considered creativity. Including, of course, the remarkable collections from the designers themselves – it is their talent and drive that ultimately pulls a show together.

From behind the scenes as well as behind her camera, Kirstin offers an unusual and eye-catching portrayal of the various elements – not all of which are immediately obvious – that together create a successful catwalk show. The book also considers the changes that the popularity of blogging and the Internet have had on the fashion industry and the ever-increasing demands that these changes place on the catwalk shows.

I hope that you enjoy this illustrated insight into our industry!

Erin O'Connor

Model, writer, broadcaster; founder, Model Sanctuary; co-founder, All Walks Beyond the Catwalk; trustee, V&A Museum

London, October 2011

ALINA ISMAILOVA
in the autumn/
winter 2010 Vivienne
Westwood Gold Label
womenswear show;
Paris, March 2010

preface

THE WORLD OF THE INTERNATIONAL catwalk show is one of immense creativity – and hard work. I feel honoured to have been part of this world for the past seven years through my work as a photographer. During this time, I have been privileged to see numerous beautiful collections come down the runway and have met a diverse cross-section of incredible, talented people from across the fashion industry.

Some of the shots in this book are very personal, and I thank the subjects for the moment in time they gave me. Although many of my photographs feature very recognizable faces, they are a much freer style of image compared to the highly polished shots that we are used to seeing on magazine covers and in editorials. They are instinctive reactions to my surroundings at the time – and, so, to moments in fashion history.

The catwalk shows are a never-ending arena of inspiration for a photographer, making them highly addictive events at which to work. There is always something new to photograph each season – a fresh face, a stunning dress, a collection that turns a new corner – as well as the anticipation of the shows to come. A great show is unforgettable, a moment in time, an inspiration and an emotion.

Through this book, I hope to provide an insight into the collaboration of skills and expertise in the many different areas of interest and input at the shows, and how these are changing and evolving over time, from the very recognizable backstage through to street style and the increasingly popular blog culture that has emerged with the proliferation of the Internet.

It is not just about fashion; it's also about the audience, the energy, the talent and the sets. It is about the longevity of some designers and the shock of the new with others. My book pays homage to the talents of the international catwalk community who come together to collaborate and celebrate fashion. I hope that I have done them justice through the unique insight I have gained over the past seven years and here showcasing some of the remarkable talent and teamwork that brings fashion to life for so many people.

And I hope that you, the reader, enjoy taking your seat in the front row.

DOROTHEA BARTH JORGENSEN in the autumn/winter 2010 Christian Dior womenswear show; Paris, March 2010

Given our intense interest in – and the press coverage of – celebrities, it should come as no surprise that the front row of most international catwalk shows reflects this trend

the **front row**

SARAH JESSICA PARKER
AND MATTHEW BRODERICK
front row at the spring/
summer 2008 Ralph Lauren
40th Anniversary womenswear
show; New York, September 2007

AN ASSOCIATION BETWEEN A DESIGNER and the right celebrity 'ambassador' can help a brand fly, while an astute choice of celebrity front row guest undoubtedly adds exclusivity and glamour to any show. The right stars in attendance will ensure a media frenzy and thereby increase the amount of publicity for the label or new collection.

The principal guests of the front row will often appear in a dramatic flurry from backstage, where they may be found chatting with the designer and mingling with the models before and sometimes after the show, reinforcing the importance of their status and their allegiance with the brand. A last-minute appearance from a big star also creates a great sense of anticipation amongst the guests already assembled: Who has the designer chosen to invite? What will they be wearing?

A crowd of photographers will rush to grab the ultimate front row shots of the celebrities in their seats seconds before the lights go down and the show begins. It is these shots that will be sent in a race to the press; the right VIP in attendance can be enough to secure a headlining article.

THE BUILD UP TO A catwalk show can vary enormously in terms of the mood and pace as the guests arrive. An overcrowded, bustling show is difficult for a front row photographer as they will have to weave through the crowd to locate the main guests, as well as try to find room to get their shots. The bigger the stars in attendance, the more security they tend to have to control the crowds that inevitably form around them. A designer's choice of venue and seating layout, too, can lead to a lack of space – which, again, makes shooting the front row difficult.

Before a show, a designer and their PR team will decide how much press coverage of their front row they want, which, in turn, determines how many photographers are permitted access. Obtaining access can also be about who a photographer shoots for; high-end publications take priority, and, the more prestigious the clients, the better the access the photographer will receive. Once in, a further challenge is the amount of time photographers have to get their shots and how accommodating the

celebrities are. If a front row guest recognizes and respects a particular photographer, they will feel happier posing for them.

Designers often dress their main guests in bespoke adaptations from the collection they are about to unveil; as well as showcasing that collection, it casts the celebrities in a central role with setting a trend and establishing the collection as one of the key looks of the season. Influential designer–celebrity partnerships include Hubert de Givenchy and Audrey Hepburn and Oleg Cassini and Jackie Kennedy; more recently, Jean Paul Gaultier worked with Madonna to create costumes, including the fêted 'cone bra', for her Blonde Ambition Tour (1990) and Confessions Tour (2006).

IN THE FRONT ROW, STARS are frequently seated together in pairs or small groups, as this works well as a feature in the magazines and newspapers. It also

SUSAN SARANDON, DEMI MOORE AND
BROOKE SHIELDS front row at the autumn/winter 2010
Donna Karan show; New York, February 2010

adds to the gossip factor, as we all want to know who was sitting next to whom, and who was wearing what. With certain celebrities, any guest that they bring may also be cause for the media to run the images of them.

Celebrities use the shows to promote their own image, too, not only through media coverage, but also by establishing and maintaining relationships within the industry, such as with designers, magazine editors, buyers and key stylists, which may lead to the stars securing cover shoots and advertising campaigns. Or, it may be that they have already secured a campaign and their front row appearance is part of the contract.

An established media face may also use an appearance at the shows to unveil a whole new look. Indeed, this new image may have been created in collaboration with a designer, and so making an appearance at their show is a mark of respect for their work.

Considering our interest in celebrity alongside the atypical attractiveness of catwalk models presents a further reason to create a star-studded front row: catwalk collections risk being perceived as unobtainable, with an almost too-perfect edge, while, as beautiful as many celebrities may be, it is somehow easier to relate to their appearance and style, not least as they tend to have more conventional body shapes and will mix and match trends to suit their style. As a result, clothes that celebrities wear become much more coveted by the general public – which is why designers understand and utilize the power their presence can have at their show.

opposite:

KAREN ELSON AND SARAH SOPHIE FLICKER front row at the autumn/winter 2008 Marc Jacobs womenswear show; New York, February 2008

right:

CLAUDIA SCHIFFER AND EVA HERZIGOVÁ front row at the autumn/winter 2009 Dolce & Gabbana womenswear show; Milan, March 2009

JULIANNE MOORE, KERRY WASHINGTON, ISABEL LUCAS AND KATIE HOLMES front row at the spring/summer 2011 Calvin Klein womenswear show; New York, September 2010

above:

JENNIFER LOPEZ front row at the spring/summer 2009 Oscar de la Renta womenswear show; New York, September 2008

opposite:

HEATH LEDGER front row at the spring/summer 2008 Marc Jacobs womenswear show; New York, September 2007

above left and right:

STUART TOWNSEND AND CHARLIZE THERON front row at the spring/summer 2009 Rag & Bone womenswear show; New York, September 2008

LENNY KRAVITZ front row at the spring/summer 2011 Alexander Wang womenswear show; New York, September 2010

right:

KEIRA KNIGHTLEY AND CLÉMENCE POÉSY front row at the spring/summer 2011 Chanel womenswear show; Paris, October 2010

opposite page, clockwise from top left:

ALEXA CHUNG front row at the autumn/winter 2010 Chanel womenswear show; Paris, March 2010

ANNA MOUGLALIS AND VANESSA PARADIS front row at the spring/ summer 2011 Chanel womenswear show; Paris, October 2010

FLORENCE WELCH front row at the spring/summer 2011 Chanel womenswear show; Paris, October 2010

CAROLINE SIEBER AND POPPY DELEVIGNE front row at the spring/ summer 2010 Chanel womenswear show; Paris, October 2009

opposite:

SCARLETT JOHANSSON front row at the autumn/
winter 2009 Dolce & Gabbana womenswear show; Milan,
March 2009

above left and right:

KATE HUDSON AND WYATT RUSSELL front row at the
autumn/winter 2009 Dolce & Gabbana womenswear
show; Milan, March 2009

KYLIE MINOGUE front row at the autumn/winter 2010
Yves Saint Laurent womenswear show; Paris, March 2010

opposite:

ESTHER CAÑADAS AND ANGELA LINDVALL front row at the spring/summer 2009 DKNY 20th Anniversary womenswear show; New York, January 2008

above left and right:

KELLY OSBOURNE AND KANYE WEST front row at the spring/summer 2011 Jil Stuart womenswear show; New York, September 2010

ANOUCK LEPÈRE AND SOLANGE KNOWLES front row at the spring/summer 2011 Jeremy Scott womenswear show; New York, September 2010

*opposite page,
clockwise from
top left:*

NAOMI WATTS at
the 'Extreme Beauty
in Vogue' exhibition
opening at the
Palazzo della
Ragione; Milan,
March 2009

RACHEL WEISZ
front row at the
spring/summer
2008 Narciso
Rodriguez
womenswear show;
New York, September
2007

**KRISTIN SCOTT
THOMAS** front row
at the spring/
summer 2006
Yves Saint Laurent
womenswear show;
Paris, October 2005

UMA THURMAN
front row at the
autumn/winter 2005
Marc Jacobs
womenswear show;
New York, February
2005

right:

DITA VON TEESE in
tents at Bryant Park
before the spring/
summer 2007 Zac
Posen womenswear
show; New York,
September 2006

"There is a delicious expectancy in the air at the shows and when that blast of music starts, before any models come out, you feel on the edge of a great surprise. "

LIELA MOSS
Lead singer, The Duke Spirit

above:

DAISY LOWE, ALICE DELLAL, PORTIA FREEMAN AND PEACHES GELDOF front row at the spring/summer 2010 Dolce & Gabbana womenswear show; Milan, September 2009

opposite:

SELMA BLAIR AND VICTORIA BECKHAM front row at the autumn/winter 2008 Marc Jacobs womenswear show; New York, February 2008

> " The most enjoyable thing is to dress up at every catwalk show, just like going to an exclusive theatre premiere. "

ANNA DELLO RUSSO
Editor-at-large and creative consultant
for Vogue *Japan*

above:

NATALIE PORTMAN front row at the autumn/winter 2010 Rodarte womenswear show; New York, February 2010

right:

CLAIRE DANES front row at the spring/summer 2011 Zac Posen womenswear show; New York, September 2010

opposite:

MARIO TESTINO AND DAPHNE GUINNESS front row at the spring/summer 2010 Gareth Pugh womenswear show; Paris, September 2009

opposite:

NATASHA POLY in the spring/summer 2009
Dolce & Gabbana womenswear show; Milan,
September 2008

above:

**PETRA NĚMCOVÁ, DITA VON TEESE AND
RÓISÍN MURPHY** front row at the
spring/summer 2009 Dolce & Gabbana
womenswear show; Milan, September 2008

MICHAEL DOUGLAS AND
CATHERINE ZETA JONES
at the spring/ summer
2006 Michael Kors
womenswear show;
New York, September 2005

right:

SHARON STONE at the spring/summer 2006 Christian Dior womenswear show; Paris, October 2005

below:

THANDIE NEWTON, LAURA BAILEY AND TWIGGY front row at the autumn/winter 2010 Stella McCartney womenswear show; Paris, March 2010

> " Being in the front row is like a thousand-and-one first nights; a seat at the opera, the ballet, the theatre. When the lights go down, you never know what is going to happen or what you are going to see. 'Encore!' 'Bravo!' "

HILARY ALEXANDER
Fashion director, The Daily Telegraph

above:

CYNTHIA NIXON front row at the autumn/winter 2007 Chaiken womenswear show; New York, February 2007

left:

KIM CATTRALL front row at the spring/summer 2006 Alice Temperley womenswear show, New York, September 2005

opposite:

SUSAN SARANDON front row at the spring/summer 2011 Donna Karan womenswear show; New York, September 2010

opposite:

DAYANA FERNANDEZ AND DEMI MOORE front row at the spring/summer 2008 Proenza Schouler womenswear show; New York, September 2007

above left and right:

JULIANNE MOORE front row at the autumn/winter 2008 Rag & Bone womenswear show; New York, February 2008

KATE BOSWORTH front row at the spring/summer 2008 Rag & Bone womenswear show; New York, September 2007

left:

GISELE BÜNDCHEN
front row at the
autumn/winter
2008 Rag & Bone
womenswear show;
New York, February
2008

*opposite page,
clockwise from
top left:*

**CHRISTY
TURLINGTON** front
row at the
autumn/winter
2008 Alice Temperley
womenswear show;
New York, February
2008

KATE MOSS front
row at the
autumn/winter
2009 Chanel
womenswear show;
Paris, March 2009

**HELENA
CHRISTENSEN** front
row at the
autumn/winter 2010
Calvin Klein
womenswear show;
New York, February
2010

**LINDA
EVANGELISTA** front
row at the
spring/summer
2006 Alexander
McQueen
womenswear show;
Paris, October 2005

opposite:

CATE BLANCHETT at the spring/summer 2009
Giorgio Armani womenswear show; Milan, September 2008

above left and right:

DUSTIN HOFFMAN AND LISA HOFFMAN front row at
the spring/summer 2008 Ralph Lauren 40th Anniversary
womenswear show; New York, September 2007

ROBERT DE NIRO AND GRACE HIGHTOWER DE NIRO
front row at the spring/summer 2008 Ralph Lauren 40th
Anniversary womenswear show; New York, September 2007

opposite:

NATALIA VODIANOVA AND MARIO TESTINO front row at
the spring/summer 2006 Yves Saint Laurent womenswear
show; Paris, October 2005

above left and right:

CLIVE OWEN front row at the autumn/winter 2010
Giorgio Armani womenswear show; Milan, February 2010

TAMARA MELLON AND CHRISTIAN SLATER front row
at the autumn/winter 2008 Halston womenswear show;
New York, February 2008

Editors travel to shows worldwide in search of each season's trends, taking inspiration from the catwalk to fill the pages of their publications with the latest fashion and beauty news

the **editors**

ANNA WINTOUR
front row at the
spring/summer 2011
Tommy Hilfiger
show; New York,
September 2010

LEADING EDITORS WILL ALWAYS BE found sitting in the front row at the catwalk shows, with perhaps the most recognizable and powerful example being Anna Wintour, editor-in-chief of American *Vogue* since 1988. Anna generally takes her seat in the front row alongside colleagues from *Vogue* or, sometimes, next to key celebrities.

Fashion editors are photographed and interviewed – frequently, both – in the front row and out and about at the shows. Their initial reactions to a designer's latest collection will be eagerly anticipated by fashion reporters and news channels, as they are often indications of future trends. The editors are thus key industry figures, and it is just as important for photographers to document their presence at the shows as it is that of the celebrities – especially if they are seated together in the front row.

Many photographers at the shows will be working alongside the editor of the publication or website for which they are shooting, and will be briefed in line with the articles and reviews on which the editorial team is working. These are sometimes pre-planned features based on certain designers, models or trends, but can also be briefs that emerge in response to what the editors are seeing and picking up on at the shows.

A FASHION EDITOR – OR EDITOR in chief, editor at large, creative director or fashion director, as they may variously be known – guides the style of a publication, website or television show through their selection of clothes, accessories, shoes and hair and beauty looks that are featured, alongside commissioning written pieces that give the publication or other media its particular character. They are also responsible for the co-ordination of photographers, designers, models and celebrities at fashion shoots.

The choices and decisions that these editors make affect all of our lives to varying degrees. Some have the power to make (and break) careers; they may choose to show their support of new, up-and-coming designers, which can be all it takes to promote their label and generate sales. Editorial shoots in magazines can be seen to significantly influence cultural definitions of male and female beauty, and so are imbued with broader, societal considerations, including diversity, minority representation and health issues. Such concerns are recognized by most magazines and editors, who can influence and promote a more positive image of the fashion industry overall.

Choices made by fashion editors can have wide-reaching effects on other industries, too: for example, because retail stores select merchandise inspired by trends dictated by other parts of the industry, even people who don't read magazines may be affected by an earlier editorial decision not only when they buy clothes but also hair and beauty products. Similarly, political messages can be perpetuated alongside fashion statements through the conscious use of certain items, such as slogan T-shirts, on shoots, with the resulting pictorials used by charities and organizations to advance awareness of their cause.

The Internet (in particular, blogs and social networking websites) enables individuals from outside of the industry to access aspects of the fashion editor's remit, collaborating and sharing opinions on style, trends and fashion gossip entirely independently of any publication's partiality or bias. However, the fashion editor's position as an industry insider means that they will always have the opportunity to, for example, work with other influential people from the media and modelling industries to publicize important issues, such as has been done with healthy eating and breast cancer awareness campaigns.

The fashion industry is undoubtedly different to that which Anna Wintour encountered when she first began her editing career at *Harpers & Queen* in 1970s' London, but its editors remain as relevant as ever – and indeed are increasingly able to use their influence to help to improve the lives of others.

opposite:

HELLE PLATOU in the spring/summer 2011 3.1 Phillip Lim womenswear show; New York, September 2010

opposite:

GRACE CODDINGTON after the autumn/winter 2011
Louis Vuitton womenswear show; Paris, February 2011

above:

**AMERICAN *VOGUE* EDITORS WITH
CANDY PRATTS PRICE** front row at the
spring/summer 2006 Yves Saint Laurent
womenswear show; Paris, October 2005

opposite:

ANDRÉ LEON TALLEY front row at the spring/summer 2006
Yves Saint Laurent womenswear show; Paris, October 2005

above left and right:

HAMISH BOWLES AND VIRGINIA SMITH front row at the
autumn/winter 2009 Dolce & Gabbana womenswear show; Milan,
February 2009

MEREDITH MELLING BURKE front row at the autumn/winter 2007
Behnaz Sarafpour womenswear show; New York, February 2007

opposite:

SOPHIA NEOPHITOU-APOSTOLOU, LISA ARMSTRONG AND ALEXANDRA SHULMAN front row at the spring/summer 2010 Alberta Ferretti womenswear show; Milan, September 2009

above left and right:

LUCINDA CHAMBERS AND KATE PHELAN front row at the autumn/winter 2009 Celine womenswear show; Paris, March 2009

NINA GARCIA AND CINDY WEBER-CLEARY front row at the autumn/winter 2009 Celine womenswear show; Paris, March 2009

ANNA PIAGGI front row
at the autumn/winter
2010 Stella McCartney
womenswear show; Paris,
March 2010

opposite:

SANTO VERSACE AND
FRANCA SOZZANI front
row at the spring/
summer 2009 Versace
womenswear show;
Milan, September 2008

opposite:

SASHA PIVOVAROVA in the spring/summer 2010 Donna Karan womenswear show; New York, October 2009

opposite:

CARINE ROITFELD AND EMMANUELLE ALT front row at
the spring/summer 2010 Blumarine womenswear show;
Milan, September 2009

above left and right:

GIOVANNA BATTAGLIA front row at the autumn/winter
2010 Giorgio Armani womenswear show; Milan, February
2010

ANASTASIA BARBIERI front row at the spring/summer 2011
Narciso Rodriguez womenswear show; New York, September
2010

"I enjoy filtering and deciphering the wealth of inspiration."

KATE LANPHEAR
Senior style director (Elle USA)

above left and right:

JAMIE PALLOT AND NICOLE PHELPS front row at the autumn/winter 2011 Jason Wu womenswear show; New York, February 2011

GLENDA BAILEY AND STEPHEN GAN front row at the autumn/winter 2011 Theory womenswear show; New York, February 2011

opposite:

JESSICA STAM in the autumn/winter 2009 Marc Jacobs womenswear show; New York, February 2009

"The most enjoyable aspect of catwalk shows is the collective exchange of ideas."

KATE LANPHEAR
Senior style director (Elle USA)

above:

JOE ZEE front row at the spring/summer 2008 Ralph Lauren 40th Anniversary womenswear show; New York, September 2007

right:

CHRISTIANE ARP front row at the spring/summer 2008 Ralph Lauren 40th Anniversary womenswear show; New York, September 2007

opposite:

ANNA DELLO RUSSO front row at the autumn/winter 2011 Narciso Rodriguez womenswear show; New York, February 2011

opposite:

IRINA LAZAREANU AND JEFFERSON HACK
front row at the autumn/winter 2010 Jeremy
Scott womenswear show; New York, February
2010

above left and right:

SUZY MENKES front row at the
spring/summer 2010 Rodarte womenswear
show; New York, September 2009

HILARY ALEXANDER front row at the
spring/summer 2011 Narciso Rodriguez
womenswear show; New York, September 2010

"The moment when a show transcends clothing and a designer's vision becomes a cadence of true beauty – that's what I enjoy seeing on the catwalk. "

JEFFERSON HACK
Co-founder, Dazed & Confused

above:

JAY ERRICO AND DANI STAHL front row at the spring/summer 2011 Rad Hourani womenswear show; New York, September 2010

left:

LUIGI TANDINI AND DAVID THIELEBEULE front row at the spring/summer 2011 Ruffian womenswear show; New York, September 2010

opposite:

ELISSEY KOSTSOV AND KATE LANPHEAR at the autumn/winter 2010 womenswear shows; Espace Ephémère Tuileries, Jardin des Tuileries, Paris, March 2010

previous page (left):

REBECCA LOWTHORPE AND STACEY DUGUID after the spring/ summer 2009 Dolce & Gabbana womenswear show; Milan, September 2008

previous page (right), clockwise from top left:

LORRAINE CANDY AND ANNE-MARIE CURTIS front row at the Giambattista Valli womenswear show; Paris, March 2010

JESS CARTNER-MORLEY front row at the autumn/winter 2010 Cerruti womenswear show; Paris, March 2010

JO ELVIN AND TRISH HALPIN front row at the autumn/winter 2010 Marni womenswear show; Milan, February 2010

PAULA REED front row at the autumn/winter 2011 3.1 Phillip Lim womenswear show; New York, February 2011

opposite:

NATASHA POLY in the autumn/winter 2010 Rick Owens womenswear show; Paris, March 2010

above left and right:

KATIE GRAND AND JEFFERSON HACK front row at the
spring/summer 2010 Diane Von Furstenberg
womenswear show; New York, September 2009

OLIVIER ZAHM AND TERRY RICHARDSON front row at
the autumn/winter 2010 Alexander Wang womenswear
show; New York, February 2010

ALICIA KUCZMAN in the autumn/winter 2010 Marc Jacobs
womenswear show; New York, February 2010

above left and right:

FRAN LEBOWITZ AND GRAYDON CARTER front row at
the spring/summer 2011 Carolina Herrera womenswear
show; New York, September 2010

STEFANO TONCHI AND LINDA WELLS front row at the
spring/summer 2011 Michael Kors womenswear show;
New York, September 2010

left:

**RIHANNA,
ROBERTA MYERS
AND NINA GARCIA**
front row at the
autumn/winter 2008
Proenza Schouler
womenswear show;
New York, February
2008

*opposite page,
clockwise from top
left:*

**CINDI LEIVE AND
JOANNA COLES**
front row at the
autumn/winter 2011
Narciso Rodriguez
womenswear show;
New York, February
2011

**ARIEL FOXMAN
AND HAL
RUBENSTEIN** front
row at the autumn/
winter 2011 Alexander
Wang womenswear
show; New York,
February 2011

**CANDY PRATTS
PRICE AND AMY
ASTLEY** front row at
the autumn/winter
2011 Derek Lam
womenswear show;
New York,
February 2011

**LUCY YEOMANS
AND VANESSA
FRIEDMAN** front row
at the spring/
summer 2008
Ralph Lauren 40th
Anniversary
womenswear show;
Central Park, New
York, September 2007

this page:

ISABELLA BLOW
front row at the
spring/summer
2006 Christian Dior
womenswear show;
Paris, October 2005

*opposite, clockwise
from top left:*

**ALIONA
DOLETSKAYA AND
SIMON ROBINS**
front row at the
spring/summer
2009 Marni
womenswear show;
Milan, September
2008

TIM BLANKS at the
spring/summer 2011
Michael Kors
womenswear show;
New York, September
2010

**ANGELICA CHEUNG
AND ELLEN VON
UNWERTH** front
row at the autumn/
winter 2010 Viktor &
Rolf womenswear
show; Paris, March
2010

GODFREY DEENY
front row at the
autumn/winter 2011
Marc by Marc
menswear and
womenswear show;
New York, February
2011

The catwalk show is now an iconic fixture in fashion history, not least for the key role it has played in the development of retail as we know it today

the **catwalk**

YULIA LOBOVA in the autumn/winter 2010 Vivienne Westwood womenswear show; Paris, March 2010

THE DATE OF THE FIRST ever catwalk show is difficult to determine, but its origins can be traced from the 'fashion parades' that took place in the couture houses of 19th-century Paris. However, it was in 20th-century USA that catwalk shows began in earnest as, after the occupation of France by German troops in 1940, it became practically impossible for designers, editors and buyers to travel to Paris to see the few shows that were still taking place there.

Fashion shows had been hosted in the USA even before the First World War. In 1903, one was held at Ehrich Brothers Emporium, New York, to entice more customers into the shop; by 1910, several other department stores had followed suit. In 1943, these events became more commonplace when a fashion publicist, Eleanor Lambert, arranged something called 'Press Week'. Influential American fashion magazines, such as *Vogue* and *Harper's Bazaar*, had previously been filled with features on European, and particularly French, fashion, but, with the launch of Press Week, editors began to take notice of American designers, featuring and crediting them more regularly in their magazines. American designs quickly became the latest trend, prompting other designers to start holding their own fashion shows in the hope of securing similar success and status.

It wasn't until the 1990s that designers began to re-think these smaller, individual shows, realizing that they would have more financial and media power collectively. In the spring of 1993, New York's first 'fashion week' was staged in the recently re-opened Bryant Park, allowing many more designers and a much larger, more international fashion crowd to gather together at a single, shared location. Decades on, an opportunity to show your collection as a new designer at one of the fashion weeks that now take place around the world can be all it takes to launch a career.

TODAY'S CATWALK SHOW IS STILL very much a commercial event, with designers often choosing to show their collections on brilliant-white, super-sleek runways. Locations for shows vary, from incredible historical buildings, such as the Grand Palais in Paris where the Chanel show is held, to a disused garage, warehouse or even a swimming pool. The choice of venue can create the perfect backdrop and atmosphere for a designer's collection, and is an important part of telling their 'story'.

Some designers still struggle with the decision to show in some of the more functional shared venues and tents at fashion weeks as they believe it does not do their collections justice or offer them any room for creativity. Likewise, there will always be designers who will choose a stark, white runway to show off a collection of brightly coloured or minimalist pieces, believing that this simplicity will ensure a strong visual impact overall and allow the clothes to speak for themselves.

The basic format of a catwalk show is often creatively interpreted by the more avant-garde or prestigious designers, who might use dancing and acting with theatrical sets and unusual lighting. Some have threaded together fantastical themes or presented shows that evoke imagery from film noir to futuristic sci fi. It is for these more creative shows that designers will generally expect the models to extend their role, such as acting in character or within a situation using more emotion, expression and movement than might be expected at the more commercial shows.

The late Alexander McQueen was famous for breaking boundaries with his breathtaking shows, which have featured fire, wind, water and snow as well as projections, robots and, in one show, live moths flying around the models. Other designers, too, have put on shows that involve water pouring like rain from above, fire billowing up through a grated runway, and snowstorms, to name but a few such spectacles. Fashion designers work with set designers and lighting engineers to achieve these incredible effects, which often cost thousands of pounds to create.

For his autumn/winter 2009 womenswear collection, designer Gareth Pugh presented his show not on a catwalk at all but as a short film, which allowed him to produce a more considered and expressive piece without having to worry about the distraction of something not going to plan in a live show, such as a model tripping on the runway.

KARLIE KLOSS in the
spring/summer 2010
Gareth Pugh
womenswear show;
Milan, September 2009

THE AVERAGE CATWALK SHOW LASTS approximately 15 to 30 minutes, during which each model will generally change outfits several times, leaving the photographers just seconds to capture each look. Before even taking a shot, though, catwalk photographers have other challenging factors to take into account. For example, as with any form of photography, lighting plays a major part in creating a great image, but the lighting chosen for each show can vary enormously – from coloured lights, spotlights and lasers to very low lighting – in order to create a particular ambience for each designer's collection. Most photographers working at the shows choose to shoot solely with the available light, so as to capture the show accurately and record the full effect of the lighting a designer has chosen to use. Shows with either minimal lighting or very bright lighting are always a challenge to shoot and photographers need to be prepared to quickly adapt to these changes. Many will shoot several shows a day, too, giving them a minimal amount of time to prepare on arrival at each venue.

As demand for coverage of the collections at the shows increases, so too does the number of photographers and film crews attending the shows – and they all vie for the most central position attainable on the podiums at the end of the runway, in order to take best advantage of the lighting set-up, but also to a get a great angle from which to shoot. Even after securing a place, there is nothing to stop a designer from changing their mind at the last minute regarding the direction in which the models will walk and the entrance from which they will first appear.

As in any industry, there is a certain hierarchy amongst the photographers and film crews; the more prestigious the clients for which they shoot, the more power they hold in terms of dictating where they would prefer to stand on the podium. Most fashion houses and designers will commission a dedicated catwalk photographer to shoot their show. As their images may be used to create a look book of the collection, and will also go on to be used for press and PR for the brand, house photographers will always be given priority on where they would like to be placed.

As well as coverage of a designer's collection shot from the head of the runway, fashion publications sometimes request additional images that capture the whole set as well as shots that play on the designer's use of lighting and other effects. Photographers may therefore work in teams, with a designated photographer at select shows moving around the venue and shooting from different positions with a wider-angle lens in order to meet this brief. Other photographers and bloggers may be working on specific projects and so will only supply this style of image as part of a feature. It is often these types of images – reaching beyond the clothes – that

The autumn/winter
2010 Christian Dior
womenswear show;
Paris, March 2010

truly depict the grandeur of a show's venue or the splendour and full extent of a designer's creativity.

Another variation on the standard catwalk format is a show that includes a celebrity appearance: singers, dancers and actors are often asked to perform next to the models, or to walk in the show modelling looks from the collection. Grace Jones was invited as a front row guest at the G-Star autumn/winter 2006 show in New York, but, halfway through, she jumped up on stage to model, dance and perform before the final curtain came down.

More recently, some designers are choosing to stream their shows live on the Internet, thereby allowing them to be viewed by an unlimited, global audience. In September 2010, Burberry announced that the launch of its new collection would be shown live in 25 of its stores. Invited customers were then able to browse the collection on iPads and place orders there and then, for delivery in seven weeks' time (the idea behind the scheme was to try to speed up the six-month cycle of buying and production).

As with its provenance, the future of the catwalk show seems uncertain – but in such a fast-paced industry, there can be no doubt that it will continue to reinvent itself as fast as the technology and creativity that define it are themselves refashioned.

Finale of the
spring/summer 2011
Marc Jacobs
womenswear show;
New York,
September 2010

"I respect so much the catwalk show; it's like the crucial 90 minutes of a football game for a World Cup tournament. "

ANNA DELLO RUSSO
Editor-at-large and creative consultant for Vogue *Japan*

KATE MOSS in the autumn/winter 2011 Louis
Vuitton womenswear show; the Louvre, Paris,
February 2011

above:

**ROSE CORDERO, MELISSA TAMMERIJN AND
SUVI KOPONEN** in the spring/summer 2011 Louis
Vuitton womenswear show; Paris, October 2010

opposite:

FREJA BEHA ERICHSEN in the autumn/winter 2010
Calvin Klein womenswear show; New York, February
2010

above:

LARA STONE in the autumn/winter 2011 Calvin Klein
womenswear show; New York, March 2011

opposite:

VLADA ROSLYAKOVA in the autumn/winter
2010 Zac Posen womenswear show; New York,
February 2010

above:

The finale of the spring/summer 2011 Jason Wu
womenswear show; New York, September 2010

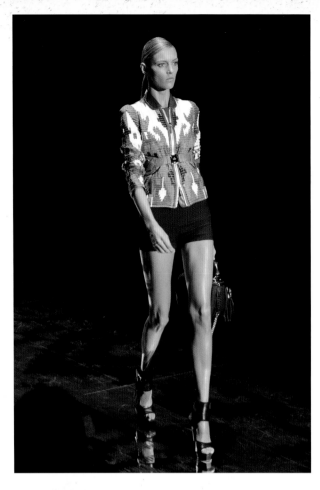

opposite page,
clockwise from
top left:

ANJA RUBIK in the
spring/summer 2010
Gucci womenswear
show; Milan,
September 2009

CARMEN KASS in
the autumn/winter
2010 DSquared2
womenswear show;
Milan, February 2010

LILY DONALDSON
in the spring/
summer 2010 Gucci
womenswear show;
Milan, September
2009

OLGA SHERER in
the autumn/winter
2010 DSquared2
womenswear show;
Milan, February 2010

this page:

JAC JAGACIAK in
the autumn/winter
2010 Viktor & Rolf
womenswear show;
Paris, March 2010

The finale of the spring/summer 2010 Dolce & Gabbana womenswear show; Milan, September 2009

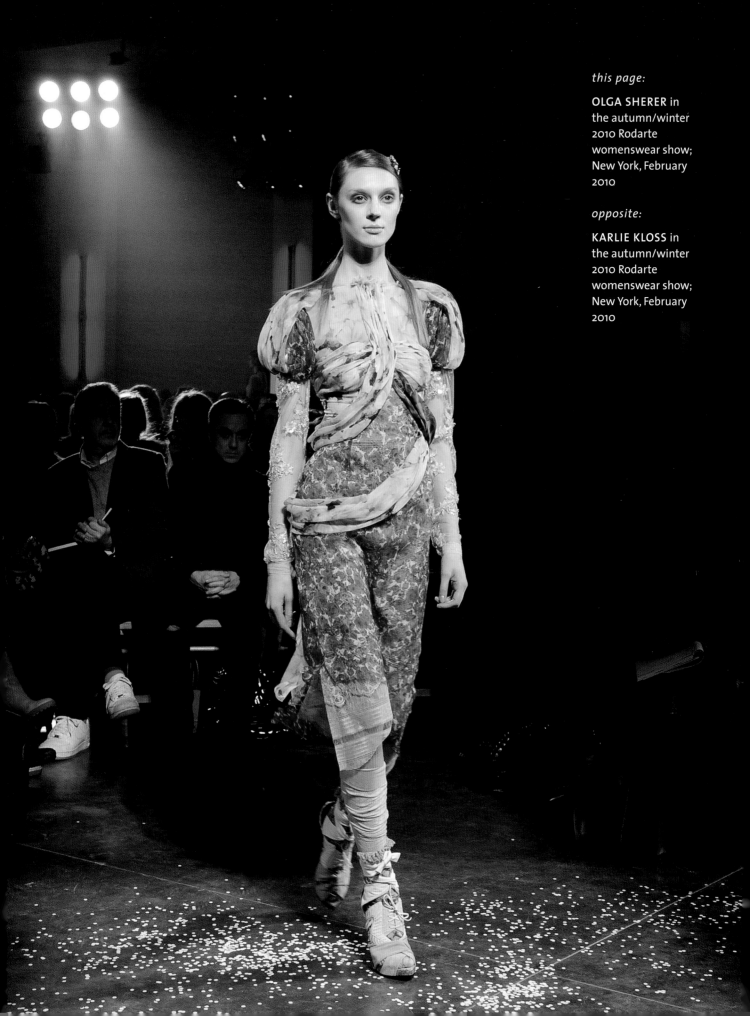

this page:

OLGA SHERER in
the autumn/winter
2010 Rodarte
womenswear show;
New York, February
2010

opposite:

KARLIE KLOSS in
the autumn/winter
2010 Rodarte
womenswear show;
New York, February
2010

opposite:

NOMA HAN in the spring/summer 2012 Walter Van
Beirendonck menswear show; Paris, June 2011

above left and right:

A model at the spring/summer 2012 Walter Van
Beirendonck menswear show; Paris, June 2011

SEBASTIAN SAUVE in the spring/summer 2012 Walter Van
Beirendonck menswear show; Paris, June 2011

opposite:

NATALIA VODIANOVA in the autumn/winter 2010
Alexander Wang womenswear show; New York, February
2010

above left and right:

ALANA ZIMMER in the spring/summer 2010 Proenza Schouler
womenswear show; New York, September 2009

MAGDALENA FRACKOWIAK in the spring/summer 2010 Proenza
Schouler womenswear show; New York, September 2009

FREJA BEHA
ERICHSEN in the
autumn/winter 2010
Chanel womenswear
show; the Grand
Palais, Paris, March
2010

this page:

FREJA BEHA ERICHSEN in the autumn/winter 2011 Alexander McQueen womenswear show; Paris, February 2011

opposite:

KINGA RAJZAK in the autumn/winter 2011 Alexander McQueen womenswear show; Paris, March 2011

above:

MICHAELA KOCIANOVA in the autumn/winter 2010
Christian Dior womenswear show; Paris, March 2010

opposite:

KSENIA KAHNOVICH in the autumn/winter 2010 Christian
Dior womenswear show; Paris, March 2010

opposite:

KSENIA KAHNOVICH in the autumn/winter 2010 Yves Saint Laurent womenswear show; Paris, March 2010

below:

ALINE WEBER in the autumn/winter 2010 Yves Saint Laurent womenswear show; Paris, March 2010

ERIN WASSON in the autumn/winter 2010 Karl
Lagerfeld womenswear show; Paris, March 2010

below:

The finale of the autumn/winter 2010 Karl Lagerfeld
womenswear show; Paris, March 2010

above:

A model in the autumn/winter 2010 Maison Martin Margiela womenswear show; Paris, March 2010

opposite:

ELLA in the autumn/winter 2010 Maison Martin Margiela womenswear show; Paris, March 2010

"The swirling vortex of the four fashion capitals is a challenge that you have to want to embrace. Dedication 24/7 means having a big love of fashion. "

ANTHEA SIMMS
Catwalk photographer

previous page:

Finale of the spring/summer 2011 Louis Vuitton
womenswear show; Paris, October 2010

opposite:

KAT HESSEN in the spring/summer 2011
Chanel womenswear show; Paris, October 2010

above:

KARLIE KLOSS in the spring/summer 2011
Chanel womenswear show; the Grand Palais,
Paris, October 2010

" The catwalk is a cabaret of talent that's addictive and which provides endless reportage opportunities **"**

ANTHEA SIMMS
Catwalk photographer

above left:

ABBEY LEE KERSHAW in the spring/summer 2010 Versace womenswear show; Milan, September 2009

above right and opposite:

VLADA ROSLYAKOVA in the spring/summer 2010 Versace womenswear show; Milan, September 2009

Countless individuals have helped to define fashion as we know it today, but certain designers stand out as true pioneers, their creativity and vision withstanding the pressures of societal and economic change as well as the test of time

the **designers**

KARL LAGERFELD
at the 'Extreme Beauty in Vogue' exhibition opening at the Palazzo della Ragione; Milan, March 2009

AFTER THE FIRST WORLD WAR, during the 1920s, French designer Gabrielle (Coco) Chanel introduced far-reaching changes to the fashion industry through her progressive designs and modernist perspective. Using influences from men's fashion in her womenswear designs, Chanel helped to change the perception of how women were expected to dress. She promoted a much more androgynous, athletic look in her daywear garments, and, through her eveningwear and 'little black dress' designs, showed women that they could be comfortable as well as sensuous and sophisticated by wearing less structured shapes than were previously available through other designers' work. In its many guises, the little black dress remains a key staple in most women's wardrobes today.

Another highly influential designer from the 1920s and 1930s was Jeanne Lanvin, who became famous for creating women's clothing that featured intricate, skilful embroidery and trimmings, often in the floral designs that would go on to become her trademark. Lanvin branched out into menswear, sportswear, lingerie and interior design, too, a then-novel approach to marketing that many fashion houses continue to follow today, as a way of allowing their brands to diversify.

In 1947, Christian Dior presented his first womenswear collection, for which he used refreshingly extravagant amounts of fabric when compared to the work of earlier designers for whom cloth had been rationed. Dior presented dresses with tiny waists, full skirts and a majestic bust, and his elegant, feminine designs greatly appealed to his post-war clientele and revamped the way that women dressed. His work was heralded as the 'new look' by Carmel Snow, *Harper's Bazaar's* editor, and helped to put Paris back on the map after the Second World War as the centre of fashion.

Towards the end of the 1950s, by means of mass production, a wealth of fashionable clothing began to be sold in standard sizes for fixed prices through retail outlets and department stores. High fashion had hit the streets, and for clothing, as with society as a whole, boundaries distinguishing superiority and value were becoming increasingly blurred. In post-war Paris, progressive designers such as Cristóbal Balenciaga, Pierre Balmain and Hubert de Givenchy were creating style sensations through tailored glamour, introducing the empire line, the tunic dress and mix-and-match separates, among other looks.

The following decade witnessed the emergence of a youth subculture that had none of the constraints or conventions of the older generations and fashion became about making a personal statement. Many of the more radical changes in fashion at this time took place in London, developing on the streets as well as through the work of up-and-coming designers. It was in the 1960s that Mary Quant became famous for launching the mini skirt and when Barbara Hulanicki founded Biba. Biba became one of the first labels to bring popular fashion to the British high street at affordable prices. Paris had its fair share of new designers, too: Yves Saint Laurent became known for his revolutionary yet elegant fashion while Emanuel Ungaro's imaginative use of colour and contrast reached out to a young audience.

FROM THE 1960S ONWARDS, WITH the help of television and a more wide-reaching fashion media, catwalk shows were being reported on all over the world, which led to Western styles going global. Paris was no longer the centre of fashion, and international designers, including Yohji Yamamoto, Kenzo Takada, Junya Watanabe, Issey Miyake and Jimmy Choo, were coming forward with their work and making a profound impact on the industry. Kenzo, in particular, became famous for using a mixture of Asian and Western influences in his unusual prints and accessories, which particularly appealed to his young customers. Yamamoto, on the other hand, was fêted as a master craftsman for the cut of his garments, and created designs that didn't really follow any trends but were more about a mood.

During the 1970s, designers continued to keep up with changes in popular culture. Vivienne Westwood, for example, is famously linked to the punk era and cited as being responsible for its visual construction through her fetishistic ranges of clothing and accessories. The punk movement also allowed London to retain a great deal of influence over fashion at the time, as it was seen to represent a direct reaction to the global financial crises that were then being endured.

VIVIENNE WESTWOOD backstage before the spring/summer 2011 Vivienne Westwood Gold Label womenswear show; Paris, October 2010

MARC JACOBS
after the spring/
summer 2012 Louis
Vuitton menswear
show; Paris, June 2011

The international fashion industry continued to extend its reach throughout the 1980s. Milan became prevalent on the scene, with the success of its ready-to-wear industry, and Italian designers such as Giorgio Armani and Nino Cerruti showed the world that fashion could be luxurious as well as practical. Armani's designs were dynamic, urban and androgynous, appealing in particular to women who were starting to take senior positions in the workplace. A new generation of urban professionals had emerged and the strength of their desire to achieve was rivalled only by their desire to look the part.

In America, Donna Karan became famous for her sexy, clinging womenswear designs that had an understated luxury; while, at the same time, Ralph Lauren had started creating aristocratic clothing for men and women at affordable prices. Lauren later branched out into sportswear and jeans, too, allowing his products to reach an even larger range of social classes and age groups.

In 1983, Karl Lagerfeld became art director at Chanel and, while still keeping within the classic Chanel remit, created much shorter cuts and more eye-catching designs than had been seen in previous collections. Prior to this, he had worked at Pierre Balmain, Jean Patou, Krizia, Charles Jourdan and Mario Valentino, and went on to join Chloe and Fendi. He eventually launched his own label Lagerfeld (for men) and Karl Lagerfeld. He has also become a leading fashion and art photographer, often shooting his own campaigns.

The economic slump of the 1990s curtailed the success of many trends emerging from the previous decade, and minimalism and simplicity became de rigueur, with designers creating far starker styles – a huge contrast to the glitz and glamour of the 1980s. New designers were suffering as a consequence of the latest financial crisis, while existing labels had to work hard to maintain their position within the industry. A brand's media presence became an integral part of ensuring its success.

However, in spite of such harsh conditions, a selection of designers still managed to shine in the 1990s. The Italian fashion house Gucci, although founded in 1921, didn't really achieve commercial success until the little-known designer Tom Ford was hired in the early part of the decade to overhaul the brand. Ford created chic and sometimes shocking clothing collections alongside numerous other product lines, and Gucci is now the one of the biggest-selling European brands in the world. Prada is another example of an Italian label established in the early part of the 20th century that didn't come into full force until the 1990s, when Miuccia Prada transformed the family-owned leather-goods manufacturer into the fashion powerhouse it is today, encompassing more than 250 stores across 65 locations worldwide.

In Milan, Gianni Versace managed to break away from the minimalist, stark styles of the decade through his gloriously colourful and glamorous womenswear collections. Similarly, Italian designers Domenico Dolce and Stefano Gabbana (Dolce & Gabbana) bucked the 1990s trends through their highly feminine, and often timeless, designs.

America boasted its fair share of emerging talent during this time, too, including Michael Kors, Marc Jacobs and Calvin Klein, all of whom remain relevant today. Having first launched his womenswear line a decade earlier, Kors hit the height of his fame in the 1990s, displaying an astute awareness and insight into trends; he produced clothing for men and women and his elegant, well-cut designs appealed to a new generation of wealthy Americans. Marc Jacobs, on the other hand, began to design with a more global market in mind; his company Marc Jacobs International launched in 1993 and, in 1997, he was appointed artistic director of the French fashion house, Louis Vuitton. His work incorporates an eclectic, energizing mix of inspirations from past and present.

Calvin Klein was at the forefront of the globalization of the fashion industry; by marketing and licensing his perfume, clothing and accessories internationally, his New York-based company survived the recession of the early 1990s. With an amazing flair for creativity and branding, Klein used a hint of eroticism to promote functional, mass-produced products, giving his designs the edge over similar products on the market and gaining them particular popularity among an increasingly affluent urban youth market.

AT THE TURN OF THE century, fashion retained something of the minimalism of the previous decade as well as a tendency to look to the past for inspiration; vintage and retro lines were increasingly popular. Eventually, though, a distinctively 21st-century style began to evolve: designers started using more colour, womenswear became ultra feminine again, brand names became ever more important, especially for the youth market, and celebrities started launching their own clothing labels.

The economic crisis began to lift and designers finally had more money to put into their collections and presentations. British designers such as the late Alexander McQueen, John Galliano and, more recently, Gareth Pugh became renowned for their elaborate catwalk shows, which incorporated aspects of the theatre and art scenes.

McQueen was celebrated for his abilities in bespoke tailoring, but his catwalk shows were legendary, too, for their extravagance and energy. He used controversial themes such as rape and violence as the basis of some of his designs, while others leaned more towards fantasy, sometimes incorporating elegant and regal elements. He worked at Givenchy before starting his eponymous label, followed in 2006 by a diffusion label, McQ. His unique talent won him British Designer of the Year four times before his premature death in 2010.

Each new season brings with it a selection of up-and-coming talent alongside existing designers who may have joined a different fashion house, be launching a new label or are simply returning to show their latest designs. The following chapter celebrates some of the world's most renowned fashion designers of recent history.

DOMENICO DOLCE, SCARLETT JOHANSSON, STEFANO GABBANA AND ORLANDO BLOOM at the 'Extreme Beauty in Vogue' exhibition opening at the Palazzo della Ragione; Milan, March 2009

left:

GIORGIO ARMANI
after the
spring/summer
2009 Giorgio
Armani
womenswear show
at the Armani
building; Milan,
September 2008

right:

ANNA ILNITSKAYA
in the autumn/
winter 2010 Giorgio
Armani womens-
wear show; Milan,
February 2010

> "Catwalk shows represent a direct dialogue with designers with their purest vision for the clothing they've designed each season."

KATE LANPHEAR
Senior style director (Elle USA)

above:

DONATELLA VERSACE AND CHRISTOPHER KANE
at the autumn/winter 2010 Versus womenswear presentation; Milan, February 2010

opposite:

MALENE KNUDSEN, MICHELLE WESTGEEST AND ALEKSANDRA TSYGANENKO in the autumn/winter 2010 Versus womenswear show; Paris, February 2010

opposite:

CAROLINA HERRERA front row at the spring/ summer 2008 Ralph Lauren 40th Anniversary womenswear show; Central Park, New York, September 2007

above left and right:

JANE KRAKOWSKI AND MICHAEL KORS backstage after the spring/summer 2008 Michael Kors womenswear show; New York, September 2007

TOMMY HILFIGER AND DEE OCLEPPO front row at the spring/summer Narciso Rodriguez womenswear show; New York, September 2006

opposite:

VLADA ROSLYAKOVA in the spring/summer 2010 Ralph Lauren womenswear show; New York, September 2009

above left and right:

RALPH LAUREN after the spring/summer 2007 Ralph Lauren womenswear show; New York, September 2006

VERA WANG AND DONNA KARAN at the spring/summer 2008 Ralph Lauren 40th Anniversary womenswear show; Central Park, New York, September 2007

VIVIENNE
WESTWOOD
and models at the
autumn/winter 2010
Vivienne Westwood
Gold Label Collection
womenswear show;
Paris, March 2010

opposite:

MIUCCIA PRADA at the 'Extreme Beauty in Vogue' exhibition opening at the Palazzo della Ragione; Milan, March 2009

above:

JESSICA STAM in the autumn/winter 2008 Prada womenswear show; Milan, February 2008

above:

JOHN GALLIANO at the autumn/winter 2010
John Galliano menswear show; Paris, January 2010

opposite:

FRANCISCO LACHOWSKI in the autumn/winter 2010
John Galliano menswear show; Paris, January 2010

> " The buzz of a catwalk show is like nothing else. Being backstage with the models all lined up, ready to walk out in your collection, feels so exhilarating. "

HENRY HOLLAND
Fashion designer

above left and right:

MATTHEW WILLIAMSON front row at the spring/summer 2009 Versace womenswear show; Milan, September 2008

ALICE TEMPERLEY backstage after the autumn/winter 2007 Temperley womenswear show; New York, February 2007

opposite:

HENRY HOLLAND AND ALEXA CHUNG front row at the spring/summer 2009 Alexander Wang womenswear show; New York, January 2008

opposite:

The autumn/winter 2010 Hermes womenswear
show; Paris, March 2010

above:

JEAN PAUL GAULTIER AND LILY COLE at the autumn/
winter 2010 Hermes show; Paris, March 2010

"Designers' work is more of an art presentation rather than a fashion show. There's nothing like watching a show where the clothes are to die for – it's an adrenaline rush."

ROCCO LEO GAGLIOTI
Presenter (FashionNewsLive.com)
and former model

above:

RICK OWENS front row at the spring/summer 2010 Gareth Pugh womenswear show; Paris, September 2009

left:

ALBER ELBAZ AND LINDA EVANGELISTA at the spring/summer 2008 Lanvin Lunch at the Rainbow Room; New York, September 2007

opposite:

SONIA RYKIEL front row at the autumn/winter 2010 Sonia Rykiel womenswear show; Paris, February 2010

opposite:

ROBERTO CAVALLI in the finale of
the spring/summer 2009 Just Cavalli
womenswear show; Milan, January
2008

below:

PHOEBE PHILO in the finale of the
autumn/winter 2010 Celine
womenswear show; Paris, March 2010

above:

ANNE SOPHIE MONRAD in the spring/summer 2010 Manish Arora womenswear show; Paris, October 2009

opposite:

MANISH ARORA and models at the spring/summer 2010 Manish Arora womenswear presentation; Paris, October 2009

opposite:

A model in the autumn/winter 2010 Marithé +
François Girbaud show; Paris, March 2010

above:

MARITHÉ AND FRANÇOIS GIRBAUD with models
at the autumn/winter 2010 Marithé + François
Girbaud womenswear show; Paris, March 2010

left:

**CARMEN HAWK AND
MILA JOVOVICH** after
the spring/summer 2007
Jovovich Hawk
presentation; New York,
September 2006

*opposite page,
clockwise from top left:*

PAM HOGG front row at
the spring/summer 2010
Gareth Pugh
womenswear show; Paris,
September 2009

JIMMY CHOO at the
London College of
Fashion MA Show;
London, January 2007

CHRISTIAN LOUBOUTIN
front row at the
autum/winter 2008
Rodarte womenswear
show; New York, February
2008

**JOHN ROCHA AND
JASPER CONRAN** at the
British Fashion Awards;
the Savoy, London,
December 2010

GWEN STEFANI
on the catwalk at the
autumn/winter 2010
L.A.M.B. womenswear
presentation; New
York, February 2010

opposite page, clockwise from top left:

DIANE VON FURSTENBERG AND MARISSA BERENSON backstage after the Diane von Furstenberg autumn/winter 2009 womenswear show; New York, February 2009

LUELLA BARTLEY AND AGYNESS DEYN at the *Teen Vogue* party for Luella Bartley at the Hotel on Rivington; New York, February 2007

RACHEL ZOE AND ALBERTA FERRETTI at the autumn/winter 2007 Philosophy presentation; New York, February 2007

KELLY KILLOREN BENSIMON AND OSCAR DE LA RENTA after the autumn/winter 2006 Oscar de la Renta womenswear show; New York, February 2006

this page:

ALEXANDER WANG before the spring/summer 2009 Alexander Wang womenswear show; New York, January 2008

“Catwalk shows represent the collaboration of a lot of creativity and vision crammed into 15 minutes of mayhem. ”

MATT LEVER
Backstage photographer

above:

ADELE MILDRED, STEPHEN JONES AND BRUNO FRISONI
front row at the spring/ summer 2010 Giles Deacon
womenswear show; Paris, October 2009

opposite:

PATRICIA VAN DER VLIET in the spring/summer 2010 Giles
Deacon womenswear show; Paris, October 2009

the **buyers**

Every catwalk audience features
buyers from all over the world

MARIGAY MCKEE
front row at the
spring/ summer
2009 Salvatore
Ferragamo
womenswear show;
Milan, September
2008

A FASHION BUYER ATTENDS SHOWS – whether on behalf of their own company or boutique, or for a long-established department store or online retailer – to select key pieces from collections for inclusion in clothing ranges tailored for their target customers. They attend the shows of established labels with which they have long-term working relationships as well as shows held by new, up-and-coming designers.

In common with fashion editors, buyers are expected to monitor trends and be aware of designers who could be the newcomer of the season or who might unveil the next big thing. Also, because they need to purchase stock six months before it goes on sale in store, buyers must be able to anticipate style trends and consumer needs; catwalk shows offer them the chance to preview all the new collections and styles, and to work closely with designers on trend reports and future predictions.

Buyers must also be adept at negotiating – and renegotiating – relationships within the industry; stocking a new label may mean that an existing brand has to be dropped, for example, even if the buyer has previously enjoyed a good working relationship with the latter brand's designer or manager. Such relationships can work both ways, of course, and exclusive or of-the-moment brands may not want too many accounts and so only agree to be stocked by specific stores deemed to have the correct clientele for their designs.

Senior buyers work closely with celebrities, too, who will come into their store for styling advice and guidance on what to buy. As a result, these buyers will often be seen chatting with familiar faces in the front row at shows, where a selection of the industry's major buyers will themselves be seated – a privilege that brings with it the focus of the media spotlight, too.

Increasingly, head buyers – often also referred to as fashion co-ordinators or fashion directors – are viewed as trendsetters in their own right and so often get photographed and interviewed, both in the front row and while out and about at the shows. Bloggers, in particular, are tuned in to the fact that the buyers have their fingers very much on the pulse of the fashion world, even to the extent that what they wear may be key indicators of future trends.

Certain buyers are regularly photographed and blogged about, and are becoming famous for their personal style and which brands they choose to wear. In turn, this helps to promote the chosen brands, and so getting the right mix of celebrities, editors and buyers to attend their show can prove critical for the designers.

BAPTISTE GIABICONI in the autumn/winter 2010 Chanel womenswear show; the Grand Palais, Paris, March 2010

> "There is always going to be a time when there is one show that moves you so greatly that you come out saying 'that's why we are in this business'."
>
> **SARAH RUTSON**
> *Buyer, Lane Crawford*

above left and right:

ROOPAL PATEL AND LINDA FARGO front row at the
spring/summer 2008 Behnaz Sarafpour womenswear
show; New York, September 2009

BETH BUCCINI AND SARA EASLEY front row at the
autumn/winter 2011 Jason Wu womenswear show;
New York, February 2011

Ca5

left:

RUTH RUNBERG after the spring/summer 2011 Rodarte womenswear show; New York, September 2010

opposite:

MO WHITE, HOLLI ROGERS AND NATALIE MASSENET after the spring/summer 2010 Donna Karan womenswear show; New York, September 2009

The finale of the
spring/summer 2011
Jil Stuart womenswear
show; New York,
September 2010

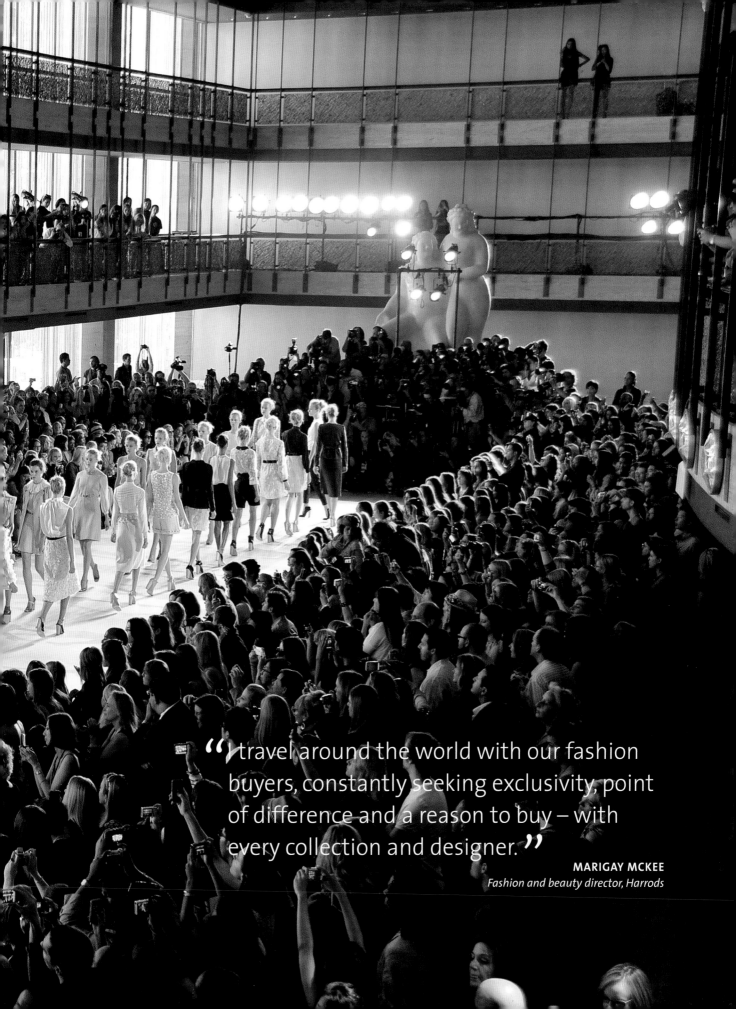

"I travel around the world with our fashion buyers, constantly seeking exclusivity, point of difference and a reason to buy – with every collection and designer."

MARIGAY MCKEE
Fashion and beauty director, Harrods

this page:

ADAM KELLY at the
spring/summer 2011
Dries Van Noten
menswear show;
Paris, June 2010

opposite:

ANITA BARR before
the autumn/winter
2009 Marni
womenswear show;
Milan, March 2009

YASMIN SEWELL
after the autumn/
winter 2010
Christian Dior
womenswear show;
Espace Ephémère
Tuileries, Jardin des
Tuileries, Paris, March
2010

opposite page,
clockwise from top
left:

AVRIL OATES front
row at the spring/
summer 2009 Dolce
& Gabbana
womenswear show;
Milan, September
2008

SIMON DOONAN
front row at the
spring/summer 2010
Rodarte womenswear
show; New York,
September 2009

AMANDA BROOKS
front row at the
spring/summer 2010
Diane von
Furstenberg
womenswear show;
New York, September
2009

MICHAEL FINK
front row at the
autumn/winter
2008 Pollini
womenswear show;
Milan, February 2008

opposite:

ANN STORDAHL AND KEN DOWNING front row at the spring/summer 2010 Marc Jacobs womenswear show; New York, September 2009

above left and right:

ERIN MULLANEY before the spring/summer 2010 Marni womenswear show; Milan, September 2009

ELIZABETH KANFER at the spring/summer 2011 womenswear shows; Lincoln Center, New York, September 2010

previous page:

The spring/summer 2010 Chanel womenswear show; the Grand Palais, Paris, 2010

opposite:

SARAH KIM before the autumn/winter 2011 Alexander Wang womenswear show; New York, February 2011

above left and right:

JULIE GILHART front row at the spring/summer 2007 Luella Bartley womenswear show; New York, September 2006

STEPHANIE SOLOMAN front row at the spring/summer 2006 Ralph Lauren womenswear show; New York, September 2005

below:

SAMA AND HAYA ABU KHADRA at the autumn/winter 2010 womenswear shows; Espace Ephémère Tuileries, Jardin des Tuileries, Paris, March 2010

opposite:

MARIA KERNER before the spring/summer 2010 Marni womenswear show; Milan, September 2009

Backstage is where the creative flourish and flair of the catwalk steps up a gear — and it can be as exhilarating to witness as the show itself

backstage

AGYNESS DEYN
backstage at the spring/summer 2008 Preen womenswear show; New York, September 2007

BEHIND THE SCENES, A PROFUSION of professionals – including camera crews, journalists and photographers – works tirelessly before, during and after the show. Leading hair stylists and make-up artists will often work closely with designers months before a show to create the perfect beauty look to complement and complete their collection – although it is not unheard of for a designer to change their mind, or change aspects of the looks, moments before a show starts.

On the day, as the models rush in from castings, fittings and previous shows, the hair stylists, make-up artists, nail technicians and dressers all work quickly to get them ready on time. Like the models, make-up artists are often booked to work at several shows a day. They work backstage with a team of assistants and are used to having to get the models ready in a very limited amount of time – whereas, for an editorial shoot, they might have the luxury of having several hours in which to complete hair and make-up.

Conversely, certain designers' shows have become famous for keeping models in hair and make-up for many hours and creating some of the most inspirational and cutting-edge looks of the season. At shows by Viktor Horsting and Rolf Snoeren (Viktor & Rolf) and Christian Dior – and, previously, John Galliano and Alexander McQueen – to name but a few, hair and make-up artists can be found utilizing anything from gold leaf, feathers, wigs or prosthetics to applying body art.

Magazines are as interested in prominent hair and beauty trends as they are in the designers' collections, and the looks on which the editors report can bring about an increase in sales of related lines within the beauty industry. Sometimes, brands will produce new products based exclusively on a sensational style or innovative look emerging from the shows, while cosmetic companies will compete with one another for the opportunity to have their products used at a show. This allows exposure through magazine reviews as well as the opportunity to ensure product-placement shots and footage. Backstage photographers and camera crews may have specific clients and projects with which they are working and so will shoot hair and make-up artists at work as they use those particular products on the models.

The designers, models, hair stylists and make-up artists will all be photographed and interviewed before, during and after the shows – which all adds to the clamour and commotion of the backstage areas. Depending on the venue a designer chooses, this area can comprise anything from a cavernous room in a grand historical setting to a narrow corridor area in a hotel. Whatever the facilities, everyone working backstage is expected to deliver a pre-eminent presentation of the designer's collection.

Photographers working behind the scenes at the shows may have a variety of briefs that they need to try and cover. It is always important to get great headshots of the hair being styled and the make-up being applied, with close-ups on any key elements such as accessories, products and tools used to create the look, as well as the technique itself. Close-ups of eyes, lips and hair will be used by magazine editors to review how a look was created.

Working backstage at the catwalk shows as a photographer offers plenty of opportunity to develop a distinctive style. Photographers are able to work directly with the models to get individual shots, as they would on a shoot. They can ask them to pose or move around in order to capture the clothing, hair and make-up at its best. These shots often have the most energy and expression in them, and, if a photographer has built up a good relationship with a model, they will feel comfortable working with them in this way to make sure they get great images.

With ever more photographers and videographers working backstage, it is increasing difficult each season for even some of the seasoned pros to get their shots, due to the lack of space and time available in which to work, so a good relationship with the models can make a significant difference. The models are generally aware of which publications certain photographers work for and also which photographers take great pictures; both factors can, of course, influence who they will be willing to spend more time with being photographed.

EKATERINA AND
INGUNA BUTANE
backstage at the
autumn/winter
2006 Wunderkind
womenswear show;
New York, February
2005

Adding to this furore backstage are the last-minute alterations that are frequently made to the garments, and designers may even pull or swap certain looks as they give their collections the final once-over before it goes down the runway. They often enlist the help of a stylist who will work with them behind the scenes and help with final decisions on anything from accessories to how the clothes should be styled; trousers and sleeves rolled up or down, how to tie belts, whether jackets should be worn open or even slung over the models' shoulders. All such finishing touches can really give a collection expression and character. Leading stylists within the industry will also work on editorials and huge advertising campaigns with designers, as well as at their shows, and are respected within the industry for their creativity and vision.

DESPITE WHAT MIGHT BE CONCLUDED from the foregoing, however, access to the backstage is always very limited, probably more so than for any other area of a catwalk event as it offers a chance to see a new collection, the hair and make-up and, sometimes, the celebrity front row guests ahead of the rest of the guests and media representatives who are waiting front of house for the show to begin. Several of the established labels are renowned for being somewhat elitist about backstage access, with passes granted only to photographers and journalists working for high-end publications and fashion channels deemed sufficiently worthy to report on the show.

Designers often hang handwritten cue boards next to the doorway through which the models step to access the runway. These boards feature notes for the models, such as reminders on which direction and route to take on the catwalk or prompts regarding the expression and mood that the designer wishes them – and so the collection – to portray, which can be anything from sexy to demure, playful to quizzical. In some cases, the models are styled according to a certain theme or character and must act out this look in order for the show to work and live up to the designer's vision and expectations.

Once a show has begun, the backstage area becomes even more hectic. As models rush back in from the catwalk and change into their next looks, photographers shoot them first in their initial looks, just as they step off the runway, and then again in their next look while they line up patiently waiting to go back out. This part of the backstage process is one to which only certain photographers may be granted access. They will also be allowed to shoot the models in the rest of the collection once the show is in full swing. The resulting images are particularly popular for use in magazines and may even be featured at full-page size to, for example, introduce new trends.

Throughout, the designer and members of the PR team will often be found overseeing the show backstage via a monitor to ensure everything is running as planned. Using headsets, they will stay in close communication with the sound and lighting operatives and other members of the team working front of house; as with any live production, timing is crucial.

After the show, selected guests and members of the media will be invited backstage to congratulate and talk to the designer about their collection. This also offers the media, in particular, an opportunity to interview industry insiders backstage and obtain reviews about the show they have just seen or helped to create.

opposite:

VAL GARLAND AND ANASTASIA KRIVOSHEEVA
backstage at the spring/summer 2011 Vivienne Westwood womenswear show; Paris, October 2010

> **"**I love the shows as they are such a hive of activity, bursting with creation and beauty.**"**
>
> ZOE TAYLOR
> *Make-up artist*

above left and right:

SASHA PIVOVAROVA backstage at the spring/summer 2009 Prada womenswear show; Milan, September 2008

GIEDRE DUKAUSKAITE backstage at the spring/summer 2009 Prada womenswear show; Milan, September 2008

opposite:

HANNA RUNDLÖF AND DOROTHEA BARTH JORGENSEN backstage at the spring/summer 2009 Prada womenswear show; Milan, September 2008

opposite:

ROSIE HUNTINGTON-WHITELEY backstage at the autumn/winter 2006 Wunderkind womenswear show; New York, February 2005

above left and right:

CLAUDIA MERIKULA backstage at the autumn/winter 2006 Wunderkind womenswear show; New York, February 2005

MARIA DVIRNIK backstage at the autumn/winter 2006 Wunderkind womenswear show; New York, February 2005

"Working backstage at the shows is always fast paced, but the room for creativity is boundless. I've worked on everything from Afros stitched by hand, fins made from wire, and hand-set wigs."

MARK HAMPTON
Hair stylist

above left:

SVIETA NEMKOVA
backstage at the autumn/winter 2007 Karen Walker womenswear show; New York, February 2007

left:

IRINA LAZAREANU AND FREJA BEHA ERICHSEN
backstage during the autumn/winter 2008 womenswear collections. Bryant Park, New York, February 2008

opposite:

TANYA DZIAHILEVA AND MAGDALENA FRACKOWIAK
backstage at the autumn/winter 2007 DKNY womenswear show; New York, February 2007

left:

TATYANA USOVA
backstage at the
spring/summer
2007 Karen Walker
womenswear show;
New York,
September 2006

right:

**MICHELLE
BUSWELL**
backstage at the
spring/summer
2006 Alexander
McQueen
womenswear show;
Paris, October 2005

opposite:

A model backstage at the spring/summer
2008 Josh Goot womenswear show; New York,
September 2007

above:

CAROLINA PANTOLIANO in the mirror
backstage at the spring/summer 2008 Josh
Goot womenswear show; New York,
September 2010

MILAGROS SCHMOLL with her dog backstage at the spring/summer 2008 Josh Goot womenswear show; New York, September 2007

above left and right:

A model backstage at the spring/summer 2008 Josh Goot womenswear show; New York, September 2007

MICHAELA KOCIANOVA backstage at the spring/summer 2008 Josh Goot womenswear show; New York, September 2007

opposite and above:

Models backstage at the autumn/winter 2008
Romeo Gilgli womenswear show; Milan,
February 2008

"Whether it's Jean Paul Gaultier, Alexander McQueen, Louis Vuitton, Yohji Yamamoto or Lanvin, the energy at the shows is always amazing."

MARK HAMPTON
Hair stylist

above:

JESSICA STAM AND JULIA STEGNER backstage at the spring/summer 2008 Preen womenswear show; New York, September 2007

opposite:

SASHA PIVOVAROVA backstage at the spring/summer 2008 Rag & Bone show; New York, September 2007

opposite:

JULES MORDOVETS backstage at the spring/summer 2011
Vivienne Westwood womenswear show; Paris, October 2010

above:

ANDREEA DIACONU AND MATHILDE FRACHON
backstage at the spring/summer 2011 Vivienne Westwood
womenswear show; Paris, October 2010

previous pages, left and right

JUANA BERGA AND CHANTAL STAFFORD-ABBOTT
backstage at the Vivienne Westwood womenswear
show; Paris, October 2010

A model backstage at the spring/summer 2011 Vivienne
Westwood womenswear show; Paris, October 2010

above:

TIMOXA TIMOSCHENKO, DANIELA MIRZAC AND ANNA MIKHAYLIK
backstage at the autumn/winter 2008 Reyes womenswear show; New
York, February 2008

opposite:

DAUL KIM backstage at the autumn/winter 2008 Reyes womenswear
show; New York, February 2008

opposite:

DANIELA KOCIANOVA AND SARA BLOMQVIST backstage
at the spring/summer 2009 Marni womenswear show;
Milan, September 2008

above:

Models backstage at the spring/summer 2009 Marni
womenswear show; Milan, September 2008

opposite:

LINDSEY WIXSON backstage at the autumn/winter 2010
United Bamboo womenswear show; New York, February 2010

above left and right:

SIMONA ANDREJIĆ backstage at the autumn/winter
2009 Chado Ralph Rucci womenswear show; New York,
February 2010

previous pages, left and right:

COCO ROCHA backstage at the autumn/winter 2007 Rag & Bone
show; New York, February 2007

TANYA DZIAHILEVA backstage after a show at the spring/summer
2008 womenswear shows; New York, September 2007

above and opposite:

JULIA SANER backstage at the
autumn/winter 2011 Chanel womenswear
show; Paris, March 2011

Haute couture to high street: as an expression of how catwalk trends are adapted and, occasionally, anticipated, street style offers an alternative insight into the world of fashion

street **style**

BRYAN BOY after the autumn/winter 2011 Louis Vuitton womenswear show; the Louvre, Paris, March 2011

OUR MULTIFACETED IDENTITIES AND MULTIMEDIA-influenced lives have created a singular desire to seek out personal fashion inspiration through a range of trends and cross-cultural references, rather than follow any one fad. Instead of pursuing paths prescribed by the industry's commercial media, street style merges multifarious lines and looks in order to express an individualized style for everyday living.

Today's technology allows journalists and editors a fresh, faster-paced response to fashion, too: they can now take photographs, as well as write and send reviews, directly from their front row seats before a show has even finished. The online presence of fashion magazines is becoming ever more important, and there is a related rise in the number of independent fashion news websites and blogs, too. These developments bring with them the expectation of instant access to the latest fashion reviews and revelations, which in turn has generated a continual need for new photographs, illustrations and impressions.

Many of the industry's magazines and websites have adopted the already-popular blogging format as a feature on their sites. Blogs tend to embrace a freer editorial style, with writers conveying their own opinions much more than they would in conventional magazine articles. Independent bloggers also post their own photographs and illustrations as well as any other work they wish to present, with some blogs concentrating solely on street style.

Some editors have established their own blogs, or contribute to a feature blog hosted on their company's website. Models, too, host blogs, recounting the international adventures and opportunities they experience as their careers unfold. Similarly, many budding fashion photographers, journalists, stylists and illustrators have been able to break into the fashion industry and get their voices heard and their work seen by an international audience through this medium.

More established street style photojournalists and bloggers follow the shows to the different fashion capitals of the world. This range of locations can give their images a very international feel, while the shows themselves offer the opportunity to photograph and interview an impressive cross-section of people across the fashion industry, from models and celebrities to top stylists and editors.

At the catwalk shows, street style blogging and street documentary has taken off to the extent that some of the leading practitioners can be seen seated among the crowd – even in the front row. In return for invitations to the shows, they will post pictures from a show itself, or of key pieces, moments and people in attendance. Such images provide a much freer form of representation, shot as they are from less conventional angles than those utilized by the photographers on the podium. In fact, this reportage style of image is becoming increasingly popular with mainstream fashion magazines and websites, and, consequently, some bloggers are being asked to guest write or supply images for high-end publications and websites, which feature their work in the same way as they would a freelance writer or photographer chosen for their specific style.

Bloggers can even report on shows without needing necessarily to step inside a catwalk venue: guests fly in from all over the world, bringing with them a wealth of fashion knowledge and up-to-the-minute designer clothing, and their diverse style and cultural backgrounds mean that there is always plenty to write about in terms of who wore what and how.

Fashion websites and blogs have bought with them a new style of reporters and journalists. Bloggers and content editors can get their imagery and impressions from the catwalk to Internet much faster than from catwalk to cover – and to a much wider audience. The photographs featured in the chapter that follows include a collection of street style shots, taken outside various international catwalk venues, of some of the more prominent names in fashion today.

opposite:

CANDICE LAKE after the autumn/winter 2011 Theory womenswear show; New York, February 2011

this page:

At the spring/
summer 2011
womenswear shows;
Lincoln Center, New
York, September
2010

opposite:

CAROLINE ISSA
after the autumn/
winter 2011 Theory
womenswear show;
New York,
February 2011

above left and right:

Giuseppe Zanotti leopard wedges before the spring/summer 2011 Louis Vuitton womenswear show; Paris, October 2010

Alexander McQueen 'Union Jack' ankle boots at the spring/summer 2009 womenswear shows; New York, January 2009

left:

Chanel belt at the autumn/winter 2011 Donna Karan Womenswear show; New York, February 2011

above:

H & M leopard clutch at
the autumn/winter 2011
womenswear shows;
New York, February 2011

right:

Alexander Wang clutch
before the
autumn/winter 2011
Louis Vuitton
womenswear show;
Paris, March 2011

opposite:

LESTER GARCIA at the autumn/winter 2011 womenswear
shows; New York, February 2011

above left and right:

DANNY at the spring/summer 2011 menswear shows;
Paris, June 2010

YU MASUI at the autumn/winter 2011 Rick Owens
menswear show; Paris, January 2011

opposite:

ELENA PERMINOVA after the autumn/winter 2010 Christian Dior womenswear show; Espace Ephémère Tuileries, Jardin des Tuileries, Paris, March 2010

above left and right:

BETTY BACHZ at the autumn/winter 2010 womenswear shows; Espace Ephémère Tuileries, Jardin des Tuileries, Paris, March 2010

LEIGH LEZARK before the autumn/winter 2010 Christian Dior womenswear show; Espace Ephémère Tuileries, Jardin des Tuileries, Paris, March 2010

opposite:

Before the spring/summer 2012 Rick Owens menswear
show; Paris, June 2011

above left and right:

YUANYI JEFF LEE at the spring/summer 2011 Louis Vuitton
menswear show; Paris, June 2010

ANDERS SOLVSTEN THOMSEN before the autumn/winter
2011 Louis Vuitton menswear show; Paris, January 2011

this page:

TAYLOR TOMASI HILL
outside the
spring/summer 2011
Alexander Wang
womenswear show;
New York, September
2010

opposite:

CAROLINE BLOMST
before the
spring/summer 2011 Dior
Homme menswear
show; Paris, June 2010

right:

Proenza Schouler
ankle boots outside
the autumn/winter
2011 Ralph Lauren
womenswear show;
New York, February
2011

below:

Leopard-print clutch
before the
spring/summer 2011
Louis Vuitton
womenswear show;
Paris, October 2010

left:

Comme des Garcons clutch at the autumn/winter 2011 Ralph Lauren womenswear show; New York, February 2011

below:

Colourful shoes and tights at the autumn/winter 2011 womenswear shows; New York, February 2011

this page:

CAROLINA ENGMAN at the spring/summer 2011 womenswear shows; Lincoln Center, New York, September 2010

opposite:

SOPHIE FAHRMAN at the spring/ summer 2011 womenswear shows; Lincoln Center, New York, September 2010

"The runway shows are what we all work towards all year round, where all the loose seams of every facet of the industry come together to form a unified whole. It is a celebration of fashion as a living, breathing, dynamic art form."

KRISTIN KNOX
Blogger

above left and right:

PREETMA SINGH at the autumn/winter 2011 womenswear shows; New York, February 2011

NADIA NAWAZ at the autumn/winter 2011 womenswear shows; New York, February 2011

opposite:

KRISTIN KNOX outside the spring/summer 2011 Donna Karan womenswear show; New York, September 2010

opposite:

ZANNA ROBERTS RASSI outside the spring/summer 2011 Ralph Lauren womenswear show; New York, September 2010

this page:

NATASHA GOLDENBERG at the autumn/winter 2011 Ralph Lauren womenswear show; New York, February 2011

left:

Before the spring/
summer 2012 Rick
Owens menswear
show; Paris, June 2011

*opposite page,
clockwise from
top left:*

PIERRE BRIGHTON
before the
spring/summer 2012
Rick Owens
menswear show;
Paris, June 2011

After the
spring/summer 2012
Jean Paul Gaultier
menswear show;
Paris, June 2011

Before the
spring/summer 2012
Rick Owens
menswear show;
Paris, June 2011

EMIL NISSEN at the
spring/summer 2011
Cerruti menswear
show; Jardin des
Plantes, Paris,
June 2010

this page:

ANNE CATHERINE FREY before the spring/summer 2012 Cerruti menswear show; Paris, June 2011

opposite:

SEUNG EUN LEE at the spring/summer 2011 menswear shows; Paris, June 2010

this page:

ULIANA SERGIENKO
at the autumn/
winter 2010
womenswear shows;
Espace Ephémère
Tuileries, Jardin des
Tuileries, Paris,
March 2010

opposite:

**TORUNN LOVISE
GULLAKSEN** at the
autumn/winter 2010
womenswear shows;
Espace Ephémère
Tuileries, Jardin des
Tuileries, Paris,
March 2010

opposite:

LEAF GREENER at the autumn/winter 2011
womenswear shows; Lincoln Center, New York,
February 2011

above left and right:

LOTTA VOLKOVA after the spring/summer 2012
Ann Demeulemeester menswear show; Paris, June 2011

Outside the autumn/winter 2011 Ralph Lauren
womenswear show; New York, February 2011

opposite:

YU MASUI after the
spring/summer 2012
Jean Paul Gaultier
menswear show;
Paris, June 2011

this page:

SUSIE LAU at the
autumn/winter 2011
womenswear
shows; the Lincoln
Center, New York,
February 2011

"I just love that I have the opportunity to observe all that happens outside the shows from my point of view and then share it through outlets such as Style.com, GQ.com and my own blog."

TOMMY TON
Blogger and photographer

above left and right:

At the spring/summer 2011 Dior Homme menswear show;
Paris, June 2010

At the spring/summer 2011 Jean Paul Gaultier menswear
show; Paris, June 2010

opposite:

CHRISTIAN at the spring/summer 2011 Dior Homme
menswear show; Paris, June 2010

> " I enjoy seeing what people decided to wear for particular shows and then capturing that for my blog. "

HANNELI MUSTAPARTA
Model, blogger, photographer

above left and right:

ELIN KLING outside the spring/summer 2011 Oscar de la Renta womenswear show; New York, September 2010

JOANNA HILLMAN at the autumn/winter 2011 womenswear shows; Lincoln Center, New York, February 2011

opposite:

HANNELI MUSTAPARTA outside the spring/summer 2011 Oscar de la Renta womenswear show; New York, September 2010

The term 'supermodel' may first have been used in the 1940s, but it wasn't part of popular parlance until the 1990s

model **style**

ERIN WASSON
before the
spring/summer 2011
Alexander Wang
womenswear show;
New York,
September 2009

> "Autumn/winter 2010 was my debut season and I had the honour of walking in Alexander McQueen's final menswear collection. It was a very emotional experience for me and like a dream come true to meet the designer in person and to be chosen to be a part of his vision as he is one of my all-time favourite designers."
>
> **DAVID CHIANG**
> *Model*

IF A MODEL BECOMES A designer's 'favourite', they may be asked to open catwalk shows or become the face of an influential campaign for clothing, beauty products and other luxury goods. Promotional work such as this can, in turn, launch a model's career, gaining them international recognition and, potentially, securing their status as a leading figure within the industry.

Lisa Fonssagrives is considered by many to have been the world's first 'supermodel'. Her career in fashion spanned the 1930s through to the 1950s, during which period she graced the cover of *Vogue* an impressive 200 times. A lot can be learnt about the different eras in fashion by considering who was chosen as a particular period's principal representative; Fonssagrives, for example, with her highly defined and angular appearance, fitted the sophisticated looks of the French fashion houses of the post-Second World War era.

The 1960s bought Twiggy, Jean Shrimpton and Veruschka to the forefront of the fashion scene, signalling an end to the feminine ideal of the 1950s. The voluptuous figure of many models used prior to this point was replaced by a more boyish look, which corresponded to the new androgynous designs of the time. Twiggy, with her fashionably short hair and large eyes, was regularly featured in mainstream publications as well as in the industry magazines. Being a model was quickly coming to be about much more than being a face of fashion; it was also about reflecting the fabric of popular culture.

Trends of the 1970s were more focussed on natural beauty and a healthy look, arguably a departure from Twiggy's thin build. It was also during this decade that models were becoming more generally recognized, and they were soon signing exclusive contracts with cosmetics companies and designers for prominent advertising campaigns. A particular model might be singled out to be the primary representative of a popular line, and many were securing lucrative deals with brands that they had been chosen to represent.

By the 1980s, fashion advertising was universal and the top models were employed to promote everything from luxury clothing brands to soft drinks and beauty products. An elite group of girls became the designers' favourites, their muses and the foremost faces of fashion. These supermodels became celebrities in their own right, launching their own clothing ranges, appearing on chat shows and some even being offered roles in films. It was no longer simply about modelling clothes: their far-reaching fame allowed them to transform their careers into multimillion-pound franchises. Some of the biggest names within this select group remain recognizable today: Linda Evangelista, Christy Turlington, Naomi Campbell, Claudia Schiffer, Cindy Crawford, Tatjana Patitz, Helena Christensen, Eva Herzigová and, a little later on, Kate Moss. The use of the latter in high-profile campaigns sparked a revival of a super-skinny look, in clear contrast to the more curvaceous supermodels whom Kate succeeded.

LILY COLE after the
spring/summer
2006 Jean Paul
Gaultier
womenswear show;
Paris, October 2005

'Heroin chic', as this 'waif' look was dubbed, attracted a lot of criticism because of the health problems it was thought to promote. Today's fashion industry is still working hard to counter this criticism, with many of its leaders and representatives backing anti-anorexia and anti-drugs campaigns.

The late 1990s marked another turning point with fashion moving from glamour to grunge, a trend that incorporated minimalism and street style. Many designers wanted their collections – and not the 'celebrity' models wearing them – to take centre stage on the catwalk once more. Magazines and advertisers started using actors and music stars, as well as models, for print campaigns, and it was becoming harder for up-and-coming models to reach the same international status as their predecessors had done.

This trend is now stronger than ever, with at least as many celebrities as models gracing the covers of various magazines, and designers continue to use big stars for their advertising campaigns. However, fashion is not without its famous faces, with today's set of 'supermodels' including high-profile representatives such as Gisele Bündchen, Erin O'Connor, Karen Elson, Lily Cole, Lara Stone and Agyness Deyn, to name but a few.

BE IT IN A CAMPAIGN or on the catwalk, a model who encapsulates a look of the moment or of a particular collection can still make a huge difference to sales. Certain models will always stand out as the faces of an era – and these are the models that make a look come alive.

In addition to being photographed for editorials and campaigns every fashion week, the models are endlessly photographed backstage, sometimes in the front row, and out and about around the shows. A growing interest in their personal style choices is emerging hand in hand with the increase in 'street style' documentary and reporting. When the models spill out of shows, as well as posing for photos, they may talk to the bloggers and journalists about the collections. If the models are still made up, there is also the opportunity to document the hair and make-up used for collection.

The number of bloggers and photographers taking shots of the models before and after the catwalk shows, outside the different venues, seems to increase every year, and there are now numerous blogs and websites dedicated solely to models in their own clothes and 'model style'. Bloggers and photographers reporting at the shows have a chance to shoot some of the world's top models wearing, often, an incredible mixture of designer, high street and vintage clothing. The fashion magazines run similar features, with certain fashion 'favourites' repeatedly written about and photographed for their individual or quirky style.

This interest in the models' own style is hardly surprising – with their professional poise and aesthetic appeal, they are liable to look good in pretty much anything. When it comes to putting an outfit together, they are often ahead of the game, too, as they have had the opportunity to see themselves photographed in many different looks styled by top designers, stylists and hair and make-up artists from all over the world. This gives many of them a strong sense of their own personal style, in terms of what suits them, as well as an in-depth knowledge of designer brands and potential hot new trends.

Models are thus more than reflections or representations of fashion; they are often responsible for setting trends themselves, a point made flesh through the enduring example of British supermodel and international trendsetter Kate Moss.

opposite page, clockwise from top left:

STELLA TENNANT after the autumn/winter 2010 Calvin Klein womenswear show; New York, February 2010

ELLE MACPHERSON after the autumn/winter 2010 Louis Vuitton womenswear show; Paris, March 2010

KARMEN KASS after the autumn/winter 2011 Louis Vuitton womenswear show; Paris, March 2011

LILY DONALDSON after the spring/summer 2010 Ralph Lauren womenswear show; New York, September 2009

left:

MING XI after the
autumn/winter 2011
Ralph Lauren
womenswear show;
New York, February 2011

below:

HANNE GABY ODIELE
after the spring/summer
2011 Alexander Wang
womenswear show; New
York, September 2010

opposite:

CHANEL IMAN after the
autumn/winter 2010
Ralph Lauren
womenswear show;
New York, February 2010

opposite:

KRISTINA ŠALINOVIĆ after the autumn/winter 2011 Theory womenswear show; New York, February 2011

opposite:

KEKE LINDGARD at the autumn/winter 2010 womenswear show; Bryant Park, New York, February 2010

left:

JAMES SMITH after the autumn/winter 2011 Louis Vuitton menswear show; Paris, June 2011

opposite:

DOUGLAS BOOTH after the autumn/winter 2011 Louis Vuitton menswear show; Paris, June 2011

"I am an anti-star, so I always enjoy shows in retrospect. The euphoria of coming off stage having rocked the catwalk was immense though!"

KATHERINE POULTON
Model and designer/art director at The North Circular

below:

CONSTANCE JABLONSKI AND SIRI TOLLERØD after the autumn/ winter 2010 Christian Dior womenswear show; Espace Ephémère Tuileries, Jardin des Tuileries, Paris, March 2010

above top:

DOROTHEA BARTH JORGENSEN after the autumn/winter 2010 womenswear show; Paris, March 2010

above bottom:

MELISSA TAMMERIJN at the autumn/winter 2010 womenswear shows; Paris, March 2010

opposite:

RUBY ALDRIDGE after the spring/summer 2011
Marc by Marc menswear and womenswear show;
New York, September 2010

above:

ANDREEA DIACONU after the autumn/winter
2010 Dolce & Gabbana womenswear show;
Milan, February 2010

this page:

NATASHA POLY at the
autumn/winter 2010
womenswear shows;
Paris, March 2010

opposite:

ANNA KUCHKINA
after the autumn/
winter 2010 Moschino
womenswear show;
Milan, February 2010

" At the autumn/winter 2011 shows, I was booked exclusively for the Dior Homme menswear show in Paris – a huge sense of achievement! "

DAVID CHIANG
Model

above left and right:

NILS BUTLER after the spring/summer 2011 John Galliano menswear show; Paris, June 2010

EMMANUEL AMORIN after the spring/summer 2012 Louis Vuitton menswear show; Paris, June 2011

opposite:

DAVID CHIANG after the spring/summer 2012 Yohji Yamamoto menswear show; Paris, June 2011

above:

VALERIA DMITRIENKO AND JULES MORDOVETS
after the autumn/winter 2011 womenswear
presentation; New York, February 2011

opposite:

FRIDA GUSTAVSSON after the autumn/winter 2010
womenswear shows; Paris, March 2010

above left and right:

ALINE WEBER after the autumn/winter 2011 Louis Vuitton
womenswear show; Paris, March 2011

DU JUAN after the autumn/winter 2011 Louis Vuitton
womenswear show; Paris, March 2011

this page:

ERIN O'CONNOR
after the spring/
summer 2012 Erdem
womenswear show,
outside the Savoy
Hotel; London,
September 2011

opposite:

AGYNESS DEYN
after the autumn/
winter 2008 Dolce &
Gabbana womens-
wear show; Milan,
February 2008

opposite:

BRUNA TENORIO
after the autumn/
winter 2011 Louis
Vuitton womens-
wear show; Paris,
March 2011

this page:

**ABBEY LEE
KERSHAW** at the
autumn/winter 2010
womenswear shows;
Espace Ephémère
Tuileries, Jardin des
Tuileries, Paris,
March 2010

opposite:

IEKELIENE STANGE after the spring/summer 2010
Jason Wu womenswear show; New York, September 2009

above left and right:

DREE HEMINGWAY after the spring/summer 2010
Giles Deacon womenswear show; Paris, October 2009

ANNA SELEZNEVA at the spring/summer 2011
womenswear shows; New York, September 2010

> " You can add a little of your own personality on the runway through movement and expression. "

DAVID CHIANG
Model

above:

THIAGO SANTOS AND LUIS BORGES after the spring/summer 2011
Kenzo menswear show; Paris, June 2010

opposite:

REID PREBENDA, TYLER RIGGS AND AJ ABUALRUB after the
spring/summer 2011 Louis Vuitton menswear show; Paris, June 2010

this page:

ELISA SEDNAOUI after the
spring/summer 2011 Rodarte
womenswear show; New York,
September 2010

opposite:

KAROLINA KURKOVA after the
spring/summer 2011 Rodarte
womenswear show; New York,
September 2010

opposite:

WILLY CARTIER after the spring/summer 2012
Jean Paul Gaultier menswear show; Paris, June 2011

above left and right:

SEAN O'PRY after the autumn/winter 2011
Louis Vuitton menswear show; Paris, June 2011

ZAKARIA KHIARE after the spring/summer 2012
Yves Saint Laurent menswear show; Paris, June 2011

select bibliography

Anon. (2009) History of models: the rise and fall of the supermodel. Modelinia [online], article no. 6855, [n.d.] 2009. Available at http://www.modelinia.com/articles; accessed February 2011.

Anon. (2010) Karl Lagerfeld [biography]. InfomatFashion [online], 4 October 2010. Available at www.infomat.com/whoswho; accessed April 2011.

Baring, L. (2009) *Norman Parkinson: A Very British Glamour*. New York: Rizzoli International Publications, Inc.

Bolton, A. (2007) *Anglomania: Tradition and Transgression in British Fashion*. New York: Metropolitan Museum of Art Publications.

Carter-Morley, J. (2009) Eyes front. *The Guardian* [online], 13 March 2009. Available at www.guardian.co.uk/lifeandstyle; accessed February 2011.

Clarke, G. (1997) *The Photograph: A Visual and Cultural History*. New York: Oxford University Press.

Craven, J. (2008) Karl Lagerfeld [biography]. *Vogue* [online], 20 April 2008. Available at www.vogue.co.uk/biographies; accessed February 2011.

Derrick, R. & Muir, R. (2002) *Unseen* Vogue: *The Secret History of Fashion Photography*. London: Little, Brown Book Group.

Derrick, R. & Muir, R. (2003) *People in* Vogue: *A Century of Portraits*. London: Little, Brown Book Group.

Derrick, R. & Muir, R. (2010) Vogue *Model: The Faces of Fashion*. London: Little, Brown Book Group.

English, B. (2007) *A Cultural History of Fashion in the Twentieth Century: From the Catwalk to the Sidewalk*. Oxford: Berg Publishers.

Fortini, A. (2006) How the runway took off: A brief history of the fashion show. *Slate* [online], article no. 2135561, 8 February. Available at www.slate.com; accessed April 2011.

Gallet, G. (2005) *Back Stage & Front Row: Gauthier Gallet Photographs*. Göttingen, Germany (Paris): Edition 7L (Steidl).

Gardiner, S. J. (2010) When did the first ever fashion show take place, and how did it start? iStylista.com [blog], article no. 398, [n.d.] 2010. Available at www.istylista.com; accessed April 2011.

Gogerly, L. (2008) *21st Century Lives: Supermodels*. London: Hodder Wayland.

Knox, K. (2010) *Alexander McQueen: Genius of a Generation*. London: A & C Black Publishers Ltd.

Koda, H. & Yohannan, K. (2009) *Model as Muse: Embodying Fashion*. New Haven Connecticut, USA: Yale University Press.

Madsen, A. (2009) *Coco Chanel: A Biography*. London: Bloomsbury Publishing Plc.

Martin, R. *et al.* (2001) *The Fashion Book*. London: Phaidon Publishing.

Palmer, A. (2009) *Dior*. London: V & A Publishing.

Picardie, J. (2010) *Coco Chanel: The legend and the life*. London: HarperCollins Publishers.

Romeika. (2007) A tribute to the original supermodels. *A Room of One's Own* [blog], 19 August 2007. Available at http://aroom-of-ones-own.blogspot.com; accessed February 2011.

Seabastian. [n.d.] The rise and fall of the supermodel. HubPages [online], [n.d.]. Available at http://hubpages.com/hub/The-Rise-and-Fall-of-the-Supermodel; accessed February 2011.

Sahner, P. (2009) *Karl Lagerfeld*. Munich, Germany: MVG Moderne Vlgs. Ges.

Starr, G. [n.d.] What is a fashion editor? eHow.com [online], article no. 4577311, [n.d.]. Available at http://www.ehow.com/about; accessed December 2010.

Wikipedia. (2011) Alexander McQueen [online], [n.d.]. Available at http://en.wikipedia.org; accessed April 2011.

Wikipedia. (2011) Buyer (fashion) [online], [n.d.]. Available at http://en.wikipedia.org; accessed December 2011.

Wikipedia. (2011) Fashion industry [online], [n.d.]. Available at http://en.wikipedia.org; accessed April 2011.

Wikipedia. (2011) Fashion show [online], [n.d.]. Available at http://en.wikipedia.org; accessed April 2011.

Wikipedia. (2011) History of fashion design [online], [n.d.]. Available at http://en.wikipedia.org; accessed February 2011.

Wikipedia. (2011) Karl Lagerfeld [online], [n.d.]. Available at http://en.wikipedia.org; accessed April 2011.

Wikipedia. (2011) Yohji Yamamoto [online], [n.d.]. Available at http://en.wikipedia.org; accessed April 2011.

Wilcox, C. (2004) *Vivienne Westwood*. London: V & A Publishing.

acknowledgements

First, special thanks to the subjects of my photographs – I can't thank each and every one of you enough for the moment in time you gave me and, consequently, for making this book possible. A big 'thank you' also to Erin O'Connor for agreeing to write its foreword.

To my dear family and friends, who have been there for me the whole time with all the encouragement to truly believe that I could make this book happen: thank you for keeping me going with the good humour and stamina I needed to see me through some very late nights, and for sharing your individual talents and knowledge to help me take my work to a higher level. This is as much your book as it is mine: Mum and Dad; Rosie Ashforth; Toby and Claire Ray; Kerry Hart; Sue Asbury; Emma Birtwistle; Ruth Daniel; and especially Ashley Hampton – I couldn't have done this without you!

Profuse gratitude and appreciation also goes to Anthea Simms and Mitchell Sams for introducing me to the incredible world of the catwalk shows and for giving me the opportunity to grow as a photographer. To all of my colleagues and friends with whom I have worked over the years at catwalk shows around the world, thank you for sharing countless wonderful moments in so many diverse situations, for helping me when I was struggling with the language, lost, and more tired than I have ever been in my life, and for teaching me not only about fashion and photography but also about myself: Victoria Adamson; Silvia Olsen; Sol Watle; Kim Western Arnold; Jessica Weber; Judith Cheek; Rosalyn Kennedy; Simon McLennan; Travis Caine Seitz; Hattie Lewis; Katy Wynn; Matt Lever; Chris Moore; Phillip Meach; Alice Bensi; Isidore Montag; Gio Staiano; Steve Eichner.

Many thanks to everyone who took the time to write a personal quote for this book: Hilary Alexander; David Chiang; Rocco Leo Gagliotti; Jefferson Hack; Mark Hampton; Henry Holland; Stephen Jones; Kristin Knox; Kate Lanphear; Matt Lever; Marigay McKee; Liela Moss; Hanneli Mustaparta; Katherine Poulton; Anna Dello Russo; Sarah Rutson; Anthea Simms; Tommy Ton; Zoe Taylor.

Thank you to the fantastic team at the Fashion and Textile Museum, London, for all their support with this project, without which I may never have had the pleasure of being able to call myself an author. Thank you for helping me to realize the potential my images had as a glimpse into a part of fashion's history: Alison Lewy; Alison McCann; Dennis Nothdruft; Zandra Rhodes – and Morag Wood, whose help proofreading this book was absolutely invaluable to me.

Thank you, too, to the team at ACC Editions for giving me this incredible opportunity and for your guidance and patience with my very first book.